A Student's Guide to BRITISH AMERICAN Genealogy

Oryx American Family Tree Series

A Student's Guide to BRITISH AMERICAN Genealogy

By Anne E. Johnson

Oryx Press
1996

Copyright 1996 by The Rosen Publishing Group, Inc.
Published in 1996 by The Oryx Press
4041 North Central at Indian School Road
Phoenix, Arizona 85012-3397

Printed and bound in the United States of America

∞ The paper used in this publication meets the minimum
requirements of American National Standard for Information
Science—Permanence of Paper for Printed Library Materials,
ANSI Z39.48, 1984.

Library of Congress Cataloging-in-Publication Data
Johnson, Anne E.
    A student's guide to British American genealogy / Anne E. Johnson.
      p.   cm. — (The Oryx American family tree)
    Includes bibliographical references and index.
    Summary: A step-by-step guide to genealogical research for
students of British American descent or those interested in British
Americans.
    ISBN 0-89774-982-0
    1. British Americans—Genealogy—Handbooks, manuals, etc.
2. British Americans—Bibliography. [1. British Americans—
Genealogy—Handbooks, manuals, etc. 2. British Americans—
Bibliography.] I. Title. II. Series.
E184.B7J64   1996
016.929′1′072—dc20   95-38165
                                                              CIP

Contents

Chapter 1
Why Trace Your Roots?

Many things add up to make you what you are. Some of those things were determined after you were born. Even simple facts like where you grew up and the kind of schooling you received can affect everything from the accent of your speech to your ideas about the world.

But what about the shape of your face and the color of your eyes? Ever wonder why you're left-handed? Or where you got your nice singing voice when neither of your parents can carry a tune?

Genealogy means "the study of origins." By tracing your origins in previous generations and getting to know some of the personalities who made up your family lines, you can learn a lot about yourself. You'll find that some of your traits are genetic. It turns out your great-grandmother was left-handed too. If you're tall but your parents are short, you may find that a couple of generations back on your father's side there's a pair of really tall siblings.

Physical traits are not the only characteristics that can be passed from one generation to the next, but experts in psychiatry and medicine don't agree on just how much of a person's emotional makeup is genetic—or at least represents traditional behavior in the family.

Do you fly off the handle easily? Have you noticed that your father is also quick to lose his temper? As you learn about your family's past, you may find many ancestors who were also a bit high-strung. There are many factors that might cause a particular personality trait to be passed on. Perhaps there is a genetic prevalence of high blood pressure or digestive problems that leads to irritability. Or perhaps quick anger has been *taught* for generations in your family as

a way of dealing with problems. Even something like your
family's traditional diet can affect emotional responses by
causing chemical changes in the body.

The genealogical search is, above all, a way to learn about
yourself. As you embark on this fascinating adventure and
begin to gather information, keep a lookout for things you
can apply to your own future. Look for common traits, and
think about emphasizing the good ones that have passed on
and trying to control the not-so-good ones so that they are
not passed on further.

Special talents might be passed from one generation to the
next, and there is evidence that some of that is genetic.
Sports prowess, a good musical ear, a sharp mind for numbers—gifts like these may have come from an ancestor, and
you might find evidence of this in your search. Even something you may not think of as a talent, such as a hilarious
sense of humor or remarkable patience or courage, may be
related to the family line.

But how can you find this out? How can you get to know
your dead relatives by looking at books in the library and
writing their names on a diagram of a tree? Well, you will be
amazed what you can learn. First of all, it doesn't all happen
in the library. You'll learn that your first step involves talking to real, live relatives to see what they have to say and
how they feel. You'll get to see some old remembrances that
once belonged to ancestors. Touch things they held dear,
read a letter in their own handwriting, and see if you don't
begin to get a sense of their living personalities.

Combine this with a knowledge of the place, time, and
circumstances in which they lived. Get a sense of what their
village, city, or farm looked like. Was your ancestor a dirt-
poor dockworker in nineteenth-century Glasgow? Then learn
about Glasgow through your ancestors' documents and
through books and movies until you can imagine the salt
spray and soot your rough-necked relative smelled every
morning. Was she a fine young lady in the early years of
Boston, sent from her London home to marry a businessman in the colonies? Find out what old Boston was like,

The harbor in Glasgow, Scotland, located on the River Clyde, might have provided work for your Scottish ancestors.

then imagine yourself wandering lonely down those cobbled streets, longing for England.

The wonderful thing about genealogy is that it does not discriminate; you don't need to have a drop of English, Welsh, or Scottish blood to do genealogical research. Using the techniques in this book, you can explore the family history of someone you're particularly interested in, such as a famous British statesman or a Scottish writer. Your report for school on Winston Churchill, for example, will stand apart from the rest if it includes some interesting remarks about his family tree.

You will get from genealogy whatever you put into it. No one pretends that preparing a family history is an easy job, or that you can find everything you're looking for. But the more you devote energy to your search and apply cleverness, humor, patience, thoroughness, and organizational skills, the more you work will be. You may be rewarded

The passengers on the historic *Mayflower* voyage prayed for good fortune as they embarked in the year 1620.

with a journey through time that would make H. G. Wells jealous.

There's no end to what you might find. Of course, most people are hoping to discover which family lines are related to theirs, or the many surprising spellings of their last name. Perhaps they'll luck into intriguing secrets involving great-uncle Bobby's discharge from the military and why fourth-cousin Mabel suddenly joined a convent in 1936. Most genealogists looking for their British roots find themselves going back to Welsh coal miners or young gentlemen from England longing for adventure in the American colonies. A few people find that they are descendants of men who signed the Declaration of Independence, or of a Pilgrim who arrived on the *Mayflower*.

Finding out who your ancestors were can change your perception of yourself by putting you in the context of your own lineage. More than one Scottish American couple have found this out. If one is from a well-off family in the "civilized" Lowlands of Scotland and the other can trace his roots to a gang of Gaelic-speaking highway robbers, you can bet there will be no end of teasing on either side. Occasionally people tracing British roots discover that they are members of nobility. Every once in a while someone finds that he or she is actually able to claim a title or pedigree. But good luck getting anyone in the United States to call you "Your Grace" or "Your Ladyship."

At least as much fun as bringing your late ancestors to life is finding your living relatives. Not many Americans know their entire living family. For many genealogists, bringing all of your kin together is a primary goal for starting a family history. To those historians, the end result of this hard work is a big annual family reunion, maybe the start-up of a family newsletter, or even the formation of a family society to keep in touch with everyone. One genealogist was rewarded at the end of her search by learning that she had over 200 living relatives in or near a small town named after one of her ancestors.

Communicating with people is an important aspect of successful family history research. You may find unknown family members. They'll probably be just as glad to be found as you are to find them. Maybe you can become pen pals with a relative of your age who lives in a very different part of the country. You could even help each other make family trees. Maybe some relatives you unearth back in Wales will invite you to come and visit.

You might also find yourself in contact with other family historians. Some will be veteran genealogists who offer you advice and shortcuts when they notice you looking a little lost at the research library. Some will be fellow novices chatting on the Internet about their search—what they've found and where they're stuck. If you place or answer a query in a genealogy magazine, you can expect to hear from other people working on branches of your own family tree. One thing about genealogists: They love to share informa-

Boston's Faneuil Hall became known as the "Cradle of Liberty" because it was a site of anti-British protests before the American Revolution. A hub of commercial activity in colonial days, it is still a popular site among Bostonians and tourists today.

tion, because they know from experience how tough it can be to find that one missing name or date.

A person with British roots will have no trouble recognizing his or her heritage in America. To start with, the language in which this book is written was brought to America by English people in the seventeenth century.

All over the United States and Canada there are millions of people with English, Scottish, and Welsh roots. Many of them celebrate their heritage in organizations. They participate in ethnic festivals or craft fairs. Some learn to play the Highland bagpipes or study medieval English morris dancing. Some attempt to master the art of cooking Welsh stews and Cornish pasties. Churches established in America by immigrants continue to celebrate their ethnic foundations. Quakers, Presbyterians, Episcopalians, Unitarians, and Methodists are some of the groups that feel particular ties to Britain, because these religions all originated there.

For those who enjoy learning by delving into books, there

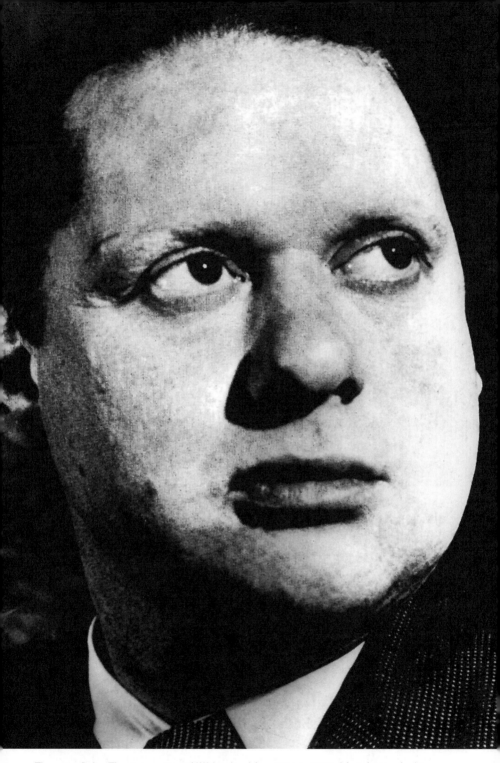

The writer Dylan Thomas, a native of Wales, lived from 1914 to 1953. He is known for his short stories, plays, and poems, as well as for his turbulent personal life.

is no end to what can be discovered about British heritage.
The linguistically inclined can adventure back through the
history of English, or tackle the endangered Celtic languages. A smattering of Scots-Gaelic, Cornish, or Welsh is
not only fun to have: It also can help with genealogy. The
literary-minded can wander among the beautiful words of
Dylan Thomas, Robert Burns, or John Keats to get a feel for
their land of origin. History buffs can let their imaginations
run wild as they experience the angry pride of Scottish clans-
men during the Jacobite rebellion, or the heartbreak of
Welsh laborers who left their families behind to seek work in
America.

Tracing family roots brings history to life. By getting to
know where you came from and meeting the individuals who
make up your past, you will learn how the vibrant culture of
a far-off land came to be part of your own American heritage.

What Is British?

This book focuses on the genealogical heritage of England,
Scotland, and Wales. These three "countries" are all members of the United Kingdom, or Great Britain. Great Britain
is a conglomerate of lands once annexed and ruled by England and now joined in a unified political system.

Besides the specific labels English, Scottish, and Welsh,
the people in the United Kingdom are collectively known as
"British." The term "Anglo" is sometimes used by British
people. Technically, it signifies only the English people of
ancient German origin. However, Anglo is sometimes used
to contrast British people with others in a certain area. In
Canada, for example, people of British heritage, rather than
indigenous or French roots, are called Anglos.

One important part of the United Kingdom omitted here
is Northern Ireland. Northern Ireland is made up of six
counties in the northernmost province of Ulster, Ireland.
These counties are part of the United Kingdom. Their
ancient Celtic population was joined by English and Scottish
immigrants in the early seventeenth century, when James I

This engraving depicts English Puritans escaping to America for a better life. The Puritans faced religious persecution in England.

of England annexed much of Ulster for the British Crown and assigned Ulster land to those loyal to him. Another large influx of Scotsmen arrived after 1695, when years of bad harvest drove them to find a better livelihood. Another twenty-six counties make up the independent Republic of Ireland. The self-rule of the Republic was won through years of struggle and bloodshed. Many in Ireland believe that Ulster rightfully belongs to the same political unit as the other twenty-six counties. This is a very complicated issue, and it may never be resolved to everyone's satisfaction. In any case, the Scottish families who stayed on in Ulster came to think of themselves as more Irish than British, and so the genealogies of Northern Ireland and the Republic of Ireland are handled together in *A Student's Guide to Irish American Genealogy*.

If you trace your roots to Britain, you may discover that

within each region a fascinating history and culture is yours to explore. For example, you may find that your ancestors came from Cornwall, a county in southwest England. In ancient times this region protected its Celtic culture against invading forces for a remarkably long time. During the Crusades it was a powerful Cornish nobleman, Richard, Earl of Cornwall, who acted as regent when the King of England was at off at war. Rich in coal, Cornwall became a major mining region during the early nineteenth century. Inevitably, the economy slumped and miners were left sick and unemployed. Many traveled to the United States then for a better life.

Not all British ancestors went directly from England, Scotland, or Wales to the United States or Canada. Britain's government began its patronage explorations in the late fifteenth century. By 1600 they had established trading companies in Canada, the Americas, the Caribbean, and India. Great Britain set up colonies on nearly every continent between the seventeenth and the early twentieth centuries. Millions of British people traveled all over the globe to outposts of the British Empire, as businesspeople, administrators, farmers, or missionaries. The intermingling of British with these many indigenous cultures makes tracing your roots to colonists an even greater adventure.

Resources

STARTING YOUR EXPLORATION

Campbell, Donald Grant, and Lerner Publications Geography. *Scotland—In Pictures.* **Minneapolis: Lerner Publications, 1991.**

Part atlas, part photo-essay, this short book tells the story of Scotland with beautiful visual images. Includes photos of urban centers, and country manors as well as poor fishing villages in the North.

Greene, Carol. *England.* **Chicago: Children's Press, 1982.**

A history of England for young people. This illustrated book begins with the invasions by Romans, Vikings, Normans, and briefly follows the rise and fall of all the monarchs.

James, Ian, and Fairclough, Chris. *Great Britain.* **New York: Franklin Watts, 1988.**

Beautifully illustrated with photographs, this book invites the young reader on a tour of historical and contemporary Britain. Includes sections on England, Scotland, Wales, the Islands, and Northern Ireland and marks cultural differences in urban and rural settings.

Llewellyn, Richard. *How Green Was My Valley.* **New York: Macmillan, 1940.**

A classic novel in which a Welsh miner's son describes the environmental and economic destruction caused by the mining economy.

Meek, James. *The Land and People of Scotland.* **Philadelphia: Lippincott, 1990.**

The young reader is taken on an illustrated journey through traditional and contemporary Scottish lifestyles. There are discussions of clans and tartans of the Highlands, the urban centers and country houses in the Lowlands, and ancient fishing culture on the Islands.

Ross, Stewart. *Where We Lived*. East Sussex, England: Wayland Publishing, 1991.

This book for young people teaches about daily English life through the ages. Examples are given from the point of view of people from many periods òf history, many professions and classes of society, and various parts of the country.

Sproule, Anna. *Great Britain*. Columbus, OH: Silver Burdett Press, 1986.

A lively view of recent history, geography, and culture, illustrated with color photos, charts, diagrams, and maps.

Sutherland, Dorothy. *Scotland*. Chicago: Children's Press, 1985.

Part of the Enchantment of the World series. Introduces students to Scotland's geographical features, history, and major cultural figures.

***Tales of the British Isles*. Bothell, WA: The Wright Group, 1992.**

A four-part series of legends, folktales, poems, and songs from England, Ireland, Scotland, and Wales. Colorfully illustrated and told in a style meant to replicate the oral tradition.

Taylor-Wilkie, Doreen. *Scotland*. Austin, TX: Steck-Vaughn, 1991.

This brief, clear history of Scotland was specially written for young adults. It begins with the unsuccessful Roman invasion of the Highlands and includes discussions of the basic monarchical feuds and the union with England.

WHY TRACE YOUR ROOTS?

Family History

This fifty-one-episode made-for-cable TV show emphasizes the fun and adventure of genealogical research while
giving practical advice. Each episode focuses on a particular aspect of genealogy, including particular heritage
searches, using archives and censuses, and computer software for family research. Available on videotape from:

Stephen Conte
P.O. Box 962
West Caldwell, NJ 07007

**Vandagriff, G. G. *Cankered Roots*. Salt Lake City, UT:
Deseret Book Co., 1994.**

A mystery novel of genealogy in action. Alexandra Campbell decides to trace her Scottish heritage, but she turns
out to be a little too good at family history research. Soon
she uncovers some things she's not supposed to know
about!

**Weitzman, David. *Underfoot: An Everyday Guide to
Exploring the American Past*. New York: Charles
Scribner's Sons, 1976.**

Where did all these people come from? Who built that?
Why do they talk like that? Learn to question your sur-
roundings and have fun finding out the answers.

**Wright, Norman E. *Preserving Your American
Heritage*. Provo, UT: Brigham Young University
Press, 1981.**

An inspiring book to send you on your way toward becoming a genealogist. Get a sense of the richness of the
heritage quilt that makes up the United States. Includes
useful information on genealogy procedure and sources,
telling you how as well as why to trace your roots.

Chapter 2
Celebrating Heritage

No matter what kind of family a person was raised in, it is common for people to become curious about their past. Many of us also have a healthy curiosity about the rest of the world. Whether your roots are in Britain, China, or Senegal, learning about your heritage will give you a new sense of self. You can also learn traditional ways of celebrating those roots.

Doing family history research can give a person a sense of belonging. You can learn where you come from and how you got here. You can make a place for yourself in history.

What if you live in a "nontraditional" family—that is, with only one parent, or perhaps with a grandparent or other relative? You may not know the name of one of your birth parents. Or, even if you know his or her name, you may have no contact with that side of the family. That doesn't mean that you can't research your roots. Doing family history research for just one side of the family is a challenging task in itself. If you find that you want to go further, perhaps you can get the information you need from the parent or relative you live with. In some cases, your genealogical project may blossom into the opportunity to reconnect with your other parent or with other relatives who weren't in your life before. If it's not possible for you to obtain information about your absent parent, your family history need not be incomplete. By working with the information you *do* have, you'll still have plenty of work on your hands and you'll have plenty to learn.

Tracing Your Roots if You Are Adopted
If you are adopted, perhaps you've never thought it possible

to trace your family history. But think about it another way: You have twice the opportunity. If you feel very close to your adoptive parents, perhaps you'd like to explore their family history (which, of course, is now your own family history as well). As you know, you don't need to be biologically related to feel part of a family. You are now a part of your adoptive family's history. By learning more about what came before you, you will feel a stronger sense of how you fit into the family.

Your other option is to trace your biological family history. This is a greater challenge, but it offers the opportunity to learn a great deal about yourself and where you come from. Psychiatrists agree that it is completely normal for adopted children to be very curious about their birth parents. How does an adopted person get information if she has never met her birth parents? If she is under eighteen, it requires legal action. The records of an adopted person's biological past are "sealed," meaning that the identities of the birth parents are legally hidden. This law is meant to protect the birth mother who doesn't want to be found and adoptive parents who don't want their adopted child to find her birth parents. It is possible, however, that your parents participated in an open adoption. While not recognized by law, an open adoption means that the adoptive parents are given some information about the birth parents and may even meet them. Rarely will they be given information about the location of the birth parents, but if you have a name and if you know the state in which you were born, you can use some of the methods in this book to begin your research.

Because birth-parent records are sealed at least until the adoptee is eighteen, it is not possible just to call up the county courthouse and get original birth certificates and other documents, as most people can. It is necessary—and best for everyone—to talk to the adoptive parents first, to see if they'll help.

An adoptive child may be able to get her feet wet in genealogy without ever actually meeting her biological mother. A minor cannot be barred from public records such as the census, so at least some clues can be gathered without having to go through legal red tape. Because adult adoptees have the extra difficulty of having to persuade officials to unseal records, it is very helpful to have some prior experience at family history research. It makes the process go a little more smoothly.

After the age of eighteen, an adopted person has legal access to biological family records in most states. Also, adult adoptees can sign up on adoption registers, and the lucky ones will be matched up with their parents if they have registered. Adoptees' rights advocacy groups all over the world are working to ease the finding of birth family information.

Adoptees who have successfully traced their roots offer some general advice to others:

- Be patient. There is no legal way (except through a medically necessitated court order) to access your birth-family records before you are eighteen. Learn whatever you can, but understand that you will have to wait for documentation.
- Be persistent. Even when you're an adult, nobody will make this search easy for you. Don't take no for an answer. Find out your legal rights from an adoptee's advocacy group, and insist that they be met.
- Don't lose hope. Every tiny bit of information is a clue that can lead to a major discovery. This is true in all kinds of family research, but even more so in an adopted search, where information is so hard to come by.
- Be grateful for any help you get. Don't expect everyone to cooperate with your search. Many roadblocks will be set up to keep you from your goal. Be sure to show your appreciation to anyone who makes your path a little easier.
- You are not alone. Most people who know that they are adopted have some interest in finding out about their past. Many books and societies can provide help.

Besides the sources listed at the end of this chapter, look for adoption support groups and service agencies in your local Yellow Pages.

Sometimes finding records on a hidden family line is a necessity. If a person is at risk for a genetic medical disorder, it may become essential to learn the medical past of the patient. Many serious illnesses tend to run from one generation to the next. These include hemophilia, Parkinson's disease, glaucoma, and muscular dystrophy. Some types of cancer are believed to be at least influenced by genetic make-up. If a doctor knows that a patient is at particular risk for high blood pressure, diabetes, or stroke, it will affect the doctor's decision to prescribe certain drugs that might increase the risk.

In order to find out about the risk of genetic diseases, a person must be able to trace the family history on both the mother's and father's sides. If there is risk of a serious medical condition, a single parent can try to trace the whereabouts of the missing parent by requesting his or her social security application from the address at the end of this chapter. If an adopted child is believed to be at risk for a serious mental or physical illness, there are ways to gain access to the sealed records. The child's doctor and guardians must apply for a court order to see what is known of the medical history of the birth parents. Only the essential documents will be unsealed.

Resources

FILM

Sean's Story: Divided Custody
Distributed by:
Films Inc.
5547 Ravenswood Avenue
Chicago, IL 60640-1199

> Sean, a child of divorced parents, learns about his family history from his grandfather.

SUPPORT FOR ADOPTEES

Adopted and Searching/Adoptee-Birthparent Reunion Registry
401 East 74th Street
New York, NY 10021
212-988-0110

Adoptees and Birthparents in Search
P.O. Box 5551
West Columbia, SC 29171
803-796-4508

Adoptees' Liberty Movement Association (ALMA)
850 Seventh Avenue
New York, NY 10019

> The foremost group in activism for adoptees' rights to information. The association set up one of the first Reunion Registries, which can be reached at 212-581-1568.

Adoptees' Search Right Association
Xenia, OH 45385
419-855-8439

Adoptees Together
Rte. 1, Box 30-B-5
Climax, NC 27233

Adoptive Families of America
3333 Highway 100 North
Minneapolis, MN 55422
800-372-3300 (24-hour hotline)

American Adoption Congress
1000 Connecticut Avenue NW
Washington, DC 20036

Concerned United Birth Parents
200 Walker Street
Des Moines, IA 50317

International Soundex Reunion Registry
P.O. Box 2312
Carson City, NV 89702

National Adoption Information Clearinghouse
11426 Rockville Pike
Rockville, MD 20852

INFORMATION ON ADOPTION

Askin, Jayne, with Molly Davis. *Search: A Handbook for Adoptees and Birthparents*, 2d ed. Phoenix, AZ: Oryx Press, 1992.

Every year adoption rights groups make more progress in establishing registers to connect adult adoptees with their biological parents. Askin offers a thorough guide to registers and searching aids in the United States.

Lifton, Betty Jean. *Lost and Found.* New York: Perennial Library, 1988.

The author was adopted and was curious about her own roots. When she became an adult, she commenced a search for her heritage. This is the story of the trials and joys she encountered as she slowly pieced together her family tree.

Marcus, Clare. *Adopted? A Canadian Guide for Adopted Adults in Search of Their Origins.* **Vancouver: International Self-Counsel Press, 1979.**

> You don't have to be Canadian to use this book. It is also useful to those born in Canada but raised in the United States, or any adoptee with Canadian relatives/ancestors. Includes registries, sealed record access rights by province, a map of archives, and clear instructions for searching.

People Searching News.

> A periodical for adoptees/birth parents, published by J. E. Carlson & Associates, P.O. Box 22611, Ft. Lauderdale, FL 33335. Phone 305-370-7100. Includes updates on adoptions, advocacy groups, birth-parent/adoptee registries, and articles by adoptees about their experiences seeking their heritage or birth family.

Savage, Thomas. *I Heard My Sister Speak My Name.* **Boston: Little, Brown, 1977.**

> The moving account of an adoptee who longs to be reunited with his birth family. Deals with his relationship with his adoptive family, his inward struggle over whether to find his biological family, and the consequences of his search.

Social Security Administration
Office of Central Records Operations
Baltimore, MD 21201

> Request form SSA-L997 to find a living relative by ordering his or her social security application. Not all requests will be honored; because this material is classified, the administration has the right to decide whether the request is warranted.

Social Security Administration Death Master File

> This record of recently deceased Americans is available in microform from Latter-day Saints Family History Centers. Check with your nearest branch. It includes millions of surnames, along with place and date of death and place of burial.

Witherspoon, Mary Ruth. "How to Conduct an Adoption Search." *Everton's Genealogical Helper*, July/Aug., 1994, p. 10.

An up-to-date essay on the difficulties and rewards of trying to find your biological family lines by a person who found some 300 living relatives. Although the author documents the discouragement she encountered from relatives and the lack of cooperation from officials, her final message is: It's worth it, so don't give up!

Chapter 3
The Land of Your Ancestors

The earliest sign of humans on the British Isles is a skull dating to 250,000 BC. The islands are believed to have been inhabited continually since then. The famous *henge* monuments, mystical arrangements of huge stones, date from about 3000 BC. By 800 BC there is evidence of a vibrant Celtic culture throughout Britain. The Celtic peoples had come from Northern Europe, and already they had established trade routes across the English Channel.

Julius Caesar, the famous Roman general, changed the course of British history when he invaded the islands in 55 BC. The Romans added Britain to their empire in 43 AD and kept control of it for the next 370 years. They defeated revolts by the resident Celts. Although they maintained a hold on southeastern and central England, they had no end of trouble with the peoples of Ireland and the Scottish Highlands.

Although the ancient Celtic culture in Britain reemerged after the Roman occupation ended, the Romans left certain legacies that must be acknowledged. In their long inhabitation of Britain they built public works such as roads and town centers. Roman roads form the foundation for highways that still cross the English and Scottish countryside. Besides the physical remains, the Romans also left a genealogical heritage in Britain. Although this was far too long ago to trace through written records, the fact that Romans settled in Britain, had children there, and intermarried with Celts had a lasting impact on the population.

The fourth century AD brought a radical change to every corner of the Roman Empire. The Emperor Constantine experienced a conversion to Christianity, a religion that had been illegal and punishable by death until Constantine's change of heart. Practically overnight, Christianity became not only acceptable but mandatory. Britain was included in this edict, and both the Roman and Celtic pagan belief systems there were largely abandoned or driven under-ground. Some Celtic traditions, however, were absorbed into British Christianity, such as the head-shaving of monks.

Over the next century the Romans lost their hold on Britain. In fact, the Roman Empire itself was in grave peril because of centuries of infighting within the government. The result in Britain was that the empire did not have the strength to withstand a new series of attacks. These came mostly from three German tribes: the Angles, the Saxons, and the Jutes, collectively known as English. By 600 AD these peoples had settled in Britain, and the Roman inhabi-tants had fled to outlying areas such as Brittany (in northern France), Wales, and Cornwall.

It was during the first centuries of English inhabitation that the various regions of Britain became separate political entities. Wessex and Mercia were the two most powerful regions in the eighth and ninth centuries, respectively. Under the leadership of their English kings, they absorbed weaker kingdoms and exercised influence over larger ones.

Cornwall, on the other hand, was a stalwart upholder of Celto-Roman culture. It was among the last places in En-gland proper to be conquered by the Germanic peoples. In the early ninth century the king of Wessex battled hard to take control of Cornwall. The Cornish, though, made allies of the recent Danish invaders. After more than a century of warfare, the Saxon King Alfred finally defeated the Danes. Fifty years later, his successors brought the regions of En-gland under one crown.

Europeans made a seemingly endless succession of raids upon Britain. Some, like the Vikings, who raided periodically from 795 to 1048, wanted at first only to plunder but later sought to settle in England. Made up of raiders from Den-mark, Sweden, and Norway, they left a strong genealogical heritage in northern England. The kings of Denmark finally

The Bayeux Tapestry (1073–1083) is one of the most famous tapestries in the world. It depicts the Norman conquest of England by William the Conqueror in 1066.

managed to gain the throne of England for a short time in the eleventh century.

The most famous invasion of Britain was made by William, Duke of Normandy (France) in 1066. He ousted the English king and took such firm control that he and his two successors established relative peace; they were the first to consolidate and organize the kingdom. The Norman invasion is sometimes said to mark the birth of the English language, as well, because it brought a Romance language into contact with the Germanic tongues spoken by the Angles and Saxons.

The Welsh—descendants of the Celtic people pushed west by the Anglo-Saxons—were not pleased with the Normans, who seized their land. Trying to save their homeland, they staged violent revolts again and again. But the Normans continued to oppress them. This period served as a model: Wales would never again be left in peace, nor would it take oppression lying down. Henry VIII had the English Parliament pass an act uniting Wales with England in 1536, but this did not stop the revolts.

In the thirteenth century a great Welsh leader named

Llewelyn ap Gruffyd became so powerful that he made an alliance with Scotsmen rebelling against English control. King Edward I of England forced Llewelyn into homage, but as soon as he returned to Wales he incited further uprisings among his people. Soon after this the famous Scottish King Robert the Bruce waged bloody warfare to protect Scotland from the invading English forces of Edward II.

The years from 1336 to 1453 are known as the Hundred Years' War. This was, in essence, a war between France and England for control of parts of France. During this same time England was being exhausted by a plague, and there was great unrest at home. Not only was England facing revolts from Wales, but the aristocracy of England was often unhappy with its own king for reasons of incompetence or favoritism to certain individuals or groups.

The discontent of the nobility was made worse by a dispute over the royal lineage. The contestants were descendants of Edward III's sons, the dukes of Lancaster and York. Henry VI suffered from dementia and was unable to govern. During his illness the Duke of York was made regent, and Lancaster's followers were livid. This sparked thirty years of civil war known as the Wars of the Roses, 1455–1485. These power struggles got their name from the badges worn by York's followers, which sported a white rose. Lancaster's side later adopted a red rose. The civil war lasted through the reigns of four kings.

The state of affairs in England in this period can be illustrated by the sordid tale of how Richard III became king. When Edward IV died in 1483, his children were in line for the throne. Richard, Duke of Gloucester, the King's brother, schemed to have Edward's children declared illegitimate and therefore not eligible to rule. The children disappeared. Legend has it that Richard had them murdered.

The Wars of the Roses ended in the Battle of Bosworth Field in 1485. Henry VII's army defeated and killed Richard III. The new dynasty was called Tudor. It was a time of strong rule and relative prosperity. The royal badge featured both a white and a red rose, in hopes of inspiring unity in the war-torn nation.

The Protestant Reformation, begun in Germany by Martin Luther, came to England in the early sixteenth century during the reign of Henry VIII. In history, this is important for the centuries of conflict it caused between Catholic and Protestant rulers in Scotland and England. Political prisoners, victims of the religious upheavals, were often sent to America. Mary, Queen of Scots, is probably the most famous character in the conflict. This Catholic queen was beheaded by order of the Protestant English Queen Elizabeth I. The Reformation marked the beginning of Presbyterianism in Scotland and the official Church of England.

In 1603 James VI of Scotland, son of Mary, Queen of Scots, became James I of England. After this, Scotland never again had a resident monarch. Scotsmen did not give up hope of independence for another century, however. Scottish nationalists wrote a document called the Covenant, which was an agreement for religious freedom stemming from the attempt of Charles I to impose bishops on the Presbyterian church of Scotland. This piece of paper became the basis for war both between Scotland and England and among the "Covenanters," who supported it to differing degrees. Civil war also erupted in England, resulting in the king's execution, the abolition of the monarchy from 1649 to 1660, and the restoration of the executed king's son. The result of this struggle was the Act of Union, which officially unified Scotland and England under the British Crown in 1707. This was the first time the term "United Kingdom" was used.

In 1760 George III became king of England. He had the bad fortune to rule during a period of obsession with democracy, played out both in the French Revolution and the American War for Independence, the event that paved the way for the ancestors of many Americans with British American roots.

The Scots have waged battles for their independence for centuries. This engraving shows a scene from the Battle of Culloden, a 1746 rebellion of Scottish Jacobites. The Jacobites, supporters of the Stuarts, the exiled royal family—were defeated by the British.

Resources

BRITAIN, HISTORY AND ATLASES

Barker, Theodore C. *A Merseyside Town in the Industrial Revolution.* **London: Frank Cass, 1993.**

The Industrial Revolution had a tremendous impact on the working class all over Great Britain. Follows the changes in the small town of St. Helens between 1750 and 1900 as its eyes are opened to new technologies and its youth are drawn away by the lure of the big city.

Bibliography of British History. **Oxford: Clarendon Press, 1928–77.**

A standard work for British history, from ancient times to 1914. Includes a partial index of periodical articles about British literature and social sciences. The bibliography can lead you to sources with more information on specific topics in British history.

Curry, Anne. *The Hundred Years War.* **Basingstoke, Hampshire, U.K.: Macmillan, 1993.**

A brief introduction to a violent period in European upheaval. Lasting from 1339 to 1453 in France, the Hundred Years War in many ways served as a bridge from the Middle Ages to the Renaissance. No part of Europe remained unaffected, and this book takes into account Britain's reactions during this era.

Dyer, James. *Ancient Britain.* **Philadephia: University of Pennsylvania Press, 1990.**

Beginning with prehistory, the reader follows the development of civilization and urbanization in Great Britain. Special treatment of the Roman inhabitation of Britain from Julius Ceasar's expedition in the first century BC.

Ellenby, Jean, and Oliver, Tim. *The Anglo-Saxon Household.* **New York: Cambridge University Press, 1986.**

The daily life of Britain's inhabitants before AD 1066. Illustrated with reconstructions of houses and other artifacts. Besides detailing building and farming methods that are known from archaeology, the book offers conjectures about family and community life before the Norman invasion.

Finnegan, Ruth, ed. *Studying Family and Community History: 19th and 20th Centuries.* **New York: Cambridge University Press, 1993.**

A four-volume series about the importance of written and oral family history in Great Britain. Includes examples from rural and urban areas and points out similarities among stories from various regions. Also considers how strictly oral history should be looked at as fact.

Foster, Janet, and Sheppard, Julia. *British Archives: A Guide to Archive Resources in the United Kingdom.* **Detroit: Gale Research, 1982.**

This book can help you find information on any aspect of British life, history, population, or culture. If you are doing genealogical research in England, this guide can help you to find documents related to your family or the history of their town.

Hakluyt, Richard. *Voyages and Discoveries.* **Ed. by Jack Beeching. New York: Penguin Books, 1982.**

A late-sixteenth-century treatise on English exploration of the world. These explorations were the precursors of the British empire, when Great Britain secured colonies all over the globe.

James, Lawrence. *The Rise and Fall of the British Empire.* **London: Little, Brown, 1994.**

Focusing on colonial expansion and its impact on administration at home, James covers British imperial history from the reign of the Stuarts (1603) into the twentieth century.

Karta Europa
7212 Fourth Street NW
Seattle, WA 98117

Can't find the historical map you need? Write to Karta for its impressive catalog. For neighborhood maps, send all the information you have about the location: town/district/shire, street address, or even if you just know some landmark your ancestor lived near.

Lloyd, Trevor Owen. *The British Empire, 1558–1983.* **London: Oxford University Press, 1984.**

Covers the glory and decline, the power and the cruelty, of the world's largest imperial force since ancient Rome. Imperial expansion is treated as a matter of political fact, and the material advantages it brought to "overtaken" peoples are mentioned along with the atrocities and the havoc it wreaked on traditional cultures all over the world.

Robson, Walter. *Britain, 1750–1900.* **London: Oxford University Press, 1993.**

A young person's guide to the making of modern Britain. Covering the time of the French and American revolutions and the Industrial Revolution, this book considers how changes in the European world view changed Britain forever.

Scoffham, Stephen; Bridge, Colin; and Jewson, Terry, eds. *U.K. Atlas.* **New York: Longman, 1991.**

A collection of detailed and wide-perspective maps of the British Isles. Includes information on climate and population.

Smith, Frank. *The Lives and Times of Our English Ancestors.* **Logan, UT: Everton Publishers, 1980.**

A two-volume study of social conditions among the working class in England leading to their massive emigration to America after the Industrial Revolution. Told specifically for genealogist readers, it includes information on records related to events.

SCOTLAND, HISTORY AND ATLASES

Dunn, Douglas, ed. *Scotland: An Anthology.* **New York: HarperCollins, 1991.**

Essays by some of the world's eminent Scottish historians on aspects of Scotland's social and political development.

Flinn, Michael. *Scottish Population History.* **New York: Cambridge University Press, 1977.**

This book follows changes in demographics in the Highlands and Lowlands. Particular periods covered are the influx of the English nobility onto Scottish land, the decades of the Industrial Revolution, and the late seventeenth century, when Scotland was struggling for independence.

Genealogical Gazetteer of Scotland

A gazetteer is a book of place-names. It is useful for pinpointing a town name you're not sure about, or checking the standard spelling. This publication is available from P.O. Box 386, Logan, UT 84321.

Grant, Eric G. *Scotland.* **World Bibliographic Series, vol. 34. Oxford, England: Clio Press, 1982.**

This huge bibliography can help you find information on everything from politics to dance. It is organized according to subject and indexed by author.

Lynch, Michael. *Scotland: A New History.* **London: Pimlico, 1992.**

A lengthy but fascinating tour through the intrigues of Scottish monarchy and wars. The book takes into account recent scholarship, reconsidering the impact of certain events, such as the Jacobite Rebellion of 1764.

Maclean, Fitzroy. *Scotland: A Concise History.* **London: Thames and Hudson, 1993.**

In less than 250 pages the author covers thousands of years of Scottish history. This is a great introduction for genealogists who would rather spent their time seeking ancestors than reading big history books. This coverage begins with prehistoric Celts and continues through the early twentieth century.

Smout, T. C. *A History of the Scottish People.* **New York: Charles Scribner's Sons, 1970.**

This ethnography includes chapters on the importance of clans, the influence of the English, and periods of civil war, poverty, and emigration.

————. *Scotland and the Sea.* **New York: Barnes and Noble, 1992.**

Beautifully illustrated, this book explores a key aspect of history for anyone studying emigration. The development of navigation and the Scots' relationship with the ocean and marine life are clues to transatlantic travel and settling patterns of Scottish ancestors.

Tomes, John. *Scotland.* **New York: Norton, 1986.**

Walk down the streets of Scotland and relive its history in this guidebook. Includes landmarks in cities, famous kirks (churches) and graveyards in the country, and a list of cultural festivals. Excellent maps by John Flower.

ENGLISH TRADITIONS AND LIFE

Charlesworth, Kate, and Cameron, Marsaili. *All That—: The Other Half of History.* **London: Pandora, 1986.**

A humorous alternative to conventional history texts, this book considers the activities and opinions of women in Great Britain, with a healthy measure of satire.

Gerard, Jessica. *Country House Life: 1815–1914.* **Oxford, England: Blackwell, 1994.**

Rural life in nineteenth-century England was a study in rich vs. poor, aristocrats vs. servants. Visit a country house and see how the classes got along. Includes excerpts from diaries and letters.

Grote, David. *British English for American Readers: A Dictionary of the Language, Customs, and Places of British Life and Literature.* **Westport, CT: Greenwood Press, 1992.**

There is no doubt that the British do not speak exactly the same language as Americans, particularly when it comes to idioms and slang. This is the perfect guide for anyone who loves British novels, television, or movies but sometimes has trouble getting the jokes.

Hole, Christina. *British Folk Customs.* **London: Hutchinson, 1976.**

From the celebration of Michaelmas to the festival of Guy Fawkes, learn about the joyous traditions of community and family in the United Kingdom. The author touches on the history, rituals, songs, food preparation, costumes, and dances of each event.

Isaacs, Alan, and Monk, Jennifer, eds. *The Cambridge Illustrated Dictionary of British Heritage.* **New York: Cambridge University Press, 1987.**

This volume seems to include every aspect of Britain and the British. Among its subjects are history, customs, development of civilization, ethnology, monarchs, colonialism, and national characteristics.

Kerridge, Roy. *Bizarre Britain: A Calendar of Eccentricity.* **New York: Blackwell, 1985.**

A month-by-month list of unusual rituals and observances of ceremonies followed in British society. Some of these practices are ancient, some rather recent. Includes maps and illustrations for locating strange festivities.

SCOTTISH TRADITIONS AND LIFE

Bennett, Margaret. *Scottish Customs: From the Cradle to the Grave.* **Edinburgh: Polygon, 1992.**

Transcriptions from taped interviews with Scottish oral historians. Not a collection of stories, but a description of habits and traditions followed in various areas of Scotland, including marriage ceremonies, initiation into a clan, and funerals. Some sections are printed in Scots-Gaelic, with English translation.

Bold, Alan Norman. *Scotland: A Literary Guide.* **London: Routledge, 1989.**

The perfect companion to classic Scottish poetry and novels, this volume explains the events and places that influenced the works of Scotland's great writers.

Bruford, Alan. *The Green Man of Knowledge and Other Traditional Tales.* **Aberdeen, Scotland: Aberdeen University Press, 1982.**

These are field recordings of traditional storytellers in Scotland. Some of the stories, from the audio tape archives of the School of Scottish Studies, University of Edinburgh, are available from no other source. Includes translations.

Cameron, Alexander Durand. *Living in Scotland, 1760–1820.* **Edinburgh: Oliver and Boyd, 1969.**

Written for young adults, this is a clear and lively description of life among all classes during this period of Scottish history. The decades covered were a time of relative prosperity in the Lowlands, brought by new farming techniques and the first dispersal of clans in the Highlands because of the sudden availability of jobs in southern cities.

Douglas, Ronald Macdonald. *Scots Book of Lore and Folklore.* **New York: Bonanza Books, 1990.**

This book is especially interesting to those searching for

their Scottish roots, because the tales are separated by clan.

Finlayson, Iain. *The Scots*. London: Oxford University Press, 1988.

This book explains national characteristics of the Scottish people. It takes into account the influence of Celtic tradition, clan loyalty, English education, and foreign input to the Scottish culture.

Griffin, Dorsey. *Silkie! Seal-Folk Tales, Ballads, and Songs*. Netarts, OR: The Griffin Press, 1985.

Silkies are Scottish mythical creatures who are human on the land and seals in the sea. A rich tradition of tales and ballads have grown up around them, from Scotland to Nova Scotia and Maine. Includes glossary.

Hallen, Arthur W. C. *Huguenots in Scotland*. London: Bowles & Sons, 1889.

One of the few thorough studies of the Huguenot population of Scotland, this is a collection of papers by members of the Huguenot Society. It deals with issues of religious persecution, where they live in Scotland, and emigration.

Harris, Paul, ed. *Scotland: An Anthology*. New York: Little, Brown, 1985.

Short classics of Scottish literature are collected in this edition.

Hayward, Brian. *Galoshins: The Scottish Folk Play*. Edinburgh: Edinburgh University Press, 1992.

Traditional Scottish drama harkens back to pre-Christian days. It is still perfomed in festivals in the northern reaches of Scotland and is seeing a revival among young people interested in their heritage. This tradition is set in the context of the daily life of the people.

Hendry, Ian D., and Graham, Stephen. *Scotscape*. Edinburgh: Oliver and Boyd, 1978.

A survey of Scottish legends and customs, spanning the whole island and hundreds of years of history. Ancient Celtic tales from the Islands accompany urban legends spun since the Industrial Revolution.

Lamont-Brown, Raymond. *Scottish Traditions and Festivals.* **Edinburgh: Chambers, 1991.**

In addition to describing traditional feasts, dances, and games, the author offers a guide for attending these events in today's Scotland.

MacDiarmid, Hugh. *Selected Poetry.* **Ed. by A. Riach and M. Grieve. New York: New Directions, 1993.**

The Scottish poet MacDiarmid wrote in the early and mid-twentieth century. This is an overview of his life's work, with commentary.

McNeill, F. Marian. *The Silver Bough.* **Edinburgh: Canongate, 1989.**

Considers the history of Scottish customs and folk wisdom. Pagan traditions continue to hold great influence, especially in rural areas of Scotland. They are combined with deeply held Christian beliefs.

Robertson, Robert Blackwood. *Of Sheep and Men.* **New York: Knopf, 1959.**

Sheep-shearing has long been an integral part of the economy and social traditions of rural Scotland. This is mainly a book of photos, capturing the pain, joy, and ageless wisdom of these weathered country dwellers. Illustrated with photos by Katherine Tweed Robertson.

Sanderson, Margaret H. B. *Mary Stewart's People.* **Tuscaloosa, AL: University of Alabama Press, 1987.**

Mary Stewart (Stuart) was Queen of Scotland from 1542 to 1567. Her life and her influence on the daily life of Scotland are discussed.

Urquhart, Fred, and Roberts, Graeme, eds. *Full Score.* **Aberdeen, Scotland: Aberdeen University Press, 1989.**

A collection of some of Scotland's finest modern short stories.

Williams, Isobel E. *Scottish Folklore.* **Edinburgh: Chambers, 1991.**

Stories of travelers, highwaymen, and ghosts from the Highlands, Lowlands, and Islands. The tales are complemented by a table categorizing them by clan.

WELSH TRADITIONS AND LIFE

Cooklin, Paul. *Michael of Wales.* **New York: Dodd, Mead, 1977.**

A book for young people describing the life and traditions of Welsh coal miners. Illustrated with photos.

Dodd, A. H. *Life in Wales.* **London: Batsford, 1972.**

A history of Wales written for young people by an eminent Welsh scholar. It focuses on households and workplaces, and how those changed as politics and technology altered Wales.

Giraldus Cambrensis. *"The Journey Through Wales"* **and** *"The Description of Wales."* **Translated by Lewis Thorpe. New York: Penguin, 1978.**

The author's name translates to "Gerald of Wales." He was a guidebook writer in about AD 1200. These two short books describe the landscape of the country and the customs of the people.

Jenkins, Philip. *A History of Modern Wales, 1536–1990.* **New York: Longman, 1992.**

Covers official unification with Britain and the periods of Welsh emigration to America. Includes excellent maps showing changing demographics and language usage. Especially strong in the political radical movement concurrent with the French Revolution.

Jones, Gwyn. *Background to Dylan Thomas, and Other Explorations.* **Oxford, England: University of Oxford Press, 1992.**

> A history of literature in Wales from the Vikings' landing to the twentieth-century poet Dylan Thomas.

Llewellyn, Sian. *Customs and Cooking from Wales.* **Swansea, Wales: Celtic Educational, 1974.**

> This is a loving celebration of traditional Welsh foods. It offers sumptuous recipes for Cambrian staples such as pasties and treacle pie, and with each dish offers a tale of its significance in daily or holiday use.

Stewart, R. J. *Celtic Gods, Celtic Goddessess.* **London: Blandford, 1990.**

> Wales was rocked by a return to druidism among radicals in the nineteenth century. This book explains some of the mysteries behind this pre-Christian religion.

Thomas, Dylan. *A Child's Christmas in Wales.* **Boston: D. Godine, 1980.**

> This is the most famous book by the most famous Welsh author. An autobiographical novel, it recalls Thomas's happy childhood days and the complexities of his relationships with members of his family. This edition features beautiful illustrations by Edward Ardizzone.

Thomas, Hugh. *A History of Wales, 1485–1660.* **Cardiff: University of Wales Press, 1972.**

> Get a running start into the history of Welsh migration to America by studying the centuries before it began. The focus is on Wales' relationship with England, including the early Norman settlement of Wales and the sixteenth-century solidification of the union.

Twenty-five Welsh Stories. **Oxford: Oxford University Press, 1992.**

> Short stories by many authors, some translated from the Welsh and some originally written in English.

BOOKS ABOUT CORNWALL

The Cornish Banner (A Baner Kernewek)

This periodical has been published since 1975 by the Cornish Nationalist Society. Its articles and letters concentrate on Celtic influence on Cornish civilization and the renaissance of Cornish culture and language.

Du Maurier, Daphne. *Rebecca.* **London: Sinclair Stevenson, 1983.**

————. *Mrs. de Winter.* **London: Sinclair Stevenson, 1984.**

These two novels examine the joys and troubles of life in Cornwall. *Rebecca* is the story of a young girl's coming of age in this traditional society, while *Mrs. de Winter* looks at the role of women, what is expected of them, their relationships with each other, and their dreams.

Peskett, Hugh. "The Problems of Cornish Genealogy." *Genealogists' Magazine,* **Vol. 17, No. 10, 1974, pp. 53–56.**

This short article sums up the best places to find information on Cornish family history and emigration, including published sources and archives. It includes a bibliography on Cornwall's history.

Rowse, A. L. *A Cornish Childhood.* **London: Jonathan Cape, 1979.**

First published in 1942, this is an autobiography of a boy from working-class Cornwall who shook his traditional ties and became an internationally renowned scholar. The self-portrait shows the author's love for his homeland—describing with joy Cornish culture and customs—even as he questions the age-old conventions of his society.

Stubbs, Jean. *Family Games.* **New York: St. Martin's Press, 1994.**

This novel finds a Cornish American genealogist tracing her family tree. The fruit of her labor, a huge family reunion, takes place in Cornwall at Christmas time and is filled with intrigue.

FILMS

The Private Life of Henry VIII, 1939.

Directed by Alexander Korda. Charles Laughton won the Academy Award for Best Actor for his portrayal of this bizarre sixteenth-century Tudor king. The movie is a comedy, focusing on Henry's obsession with fathering an heir to the throne.

The Stars Look Down, 1940.

Directed by Carol Reed. Michael Redgrave stars as David Fenwick, a young man who longs to leave his Northumbrian mining town and get a university education in the city. Thwarted in his plans by an unfortunate romance, he turns his talents to the cause of the local miners, fighting to defend them against union officers' exploitation.

How Green Was My Valley, 1941.

Directed by John Ford. This moving story of the rise and fall of a Welsh coal-mining town won Oscars for best picture and best director. It features Roddy MacDowell, in his first movie role, as a boy who witnesses how strikes and unemployment cause both his community and his family to disintegrate over the years. Also starring Walter Pidgeon and Maureen O'Hara.

Major Barbara, 1941.

Directed by Gabriel Pascal. Based on a George Bernard Shaw play, this is a story of the concept of charity and its puritanical roots in England. Barbara (Wendy Hiller), an officer in the Salvation Army, runs into a moral dilemma when the fate of her organization hangs on the generosity of a liquor manufacturer. Also starring Rex Harrison.

Great Expectations, 1946.

Directed by David Lean. This is the finest of the four film adaptations of Charles Dickens's novel. It follows the maturing of an orphan boy named Pip. As a child, Pip is sent to live with the strange, ancient Miss Havisham and her haughty ward. One day he learns that an anonymous donor has left him money if he will move to London and apprentice to a trade. Over the years he learns that goodness of the heart is greater wealth than gold.

Whiskey Galore, 1949.

Directed by Michael Balcon. This is worth seeing especially for its rare treatment of traditional life in the Isle of Eriskay in the Outer Hebrides, Scotland. The story is based on a strange but real event: during World War II a cargo ship is wrecked off this little island, spilling 50,000 cases of Scotch whiskey into the sea. Tradition (in the form of the villagers risking life and limb to retrieve the whiskey) is pitted against cold modern regulation (a man from the government is sent to round up the cargo). The satire is deepened when the villagers find themselves at odds with their own Calvinist heritage: On the Sabbath, a strict day of rest, they lose a precious day for collecting the liquor.

Richard III, 1955.

Directed by and starring Sir Laurence Olivier. Richard III was King of England only from 1483 to 1485, yet that short tenure was enough to inspire Shakespeare to write a play about him. After all, he gained his crown by killing the legitimate child heir to the throne, Edward V. Also starring Sir John Gielgud and Claire Bloom.

Tunes of Glory, 1960.

Directed by Ronald Neame. The title tunes are military tattoos played on bagpipes in the isolated peacetime camp of a Scottish Highland regiment. With brilliant performances by Alec Guinness, Susannah York, and John Mills, this is the story of quiet psychological warfare between two officers; when their enemy is at bay, they seem to have no choice but to challenge each other.

Tom Jones, 1963.

Directed by Tony Richardson. Albert Finney, Susannah York, and Dame Edith Evans star in this outrageous reenactment of Henry Fielding's eighteenth-century novel of English manners. Tom Jones was found on a doorstep and raised by a loving father into a mischievous but big-hearted young man. He finds himself at odds, however, with his adoptive brother, the sniveling, inheritance-obsessed Blifil.

A Hard Day's Night, 1964.

Directed by Richard Lester. Before the Beatles hit the scene, Britain hadn't had so much sway over America since the days of George III. The Liverpool lads do London in this smash-hit encomium to rock 'n' roll and England's coming of age. Featuring Beatles' music, of course, *A Hard Day's Night* is both romping fun and a skillful exploration of cinematic surrealism.

The Whisperers, 1967.

Directed by Bryan Forbes. Dame Edith Evans plays the elderly widow Mrs. Ross in this bleak look at the state of social ills in urban Britain. Without pretending to offer an answer, the film considers modern urban life's tragic break from ancient rural tradition that would have guaranteed an elderly person care and respect in her last days. Instead, Mrs. Ross is abandoned and penniless and learns to have enormous gratitude for any kindness toward her.

The Bostonians, 1984.

Directed by James Ivory. Vanessa Redgrave and Christopher Reeve star in this richly colored film adaptation of Henry James's novel. Although the story takes place in turn-of-the-century Boston, the money-based family feuds and class consciousness are the result of centuries of tradition, beginning with the first British settlement of Massachussetts Bay Colony in the seventeenth century.

A Passage to India, 1985.

Directed by David Lean. Based on an E. M. Forster novel, this spectacle explores the ironies of colonial racism in India during the early twentieth century. A young Indian doctor (Victor Banjeree) is accused of molesting a British woman (Judy Davis), but the charges seem to spring from the British fear of racial interaction rather than from provable events.

Howard's End, 1992.

Directed by James Ivory. One of the celebrated Merchant Ivory productions based on E. M. Forster novels, *Howard's End* is a lush recounting of class struggle. Instead of traditional rich against poor, this story takes place within the middle class. Fine acting by Vanessa Redgrave, Emma Thompson, and Anthony Hopkins and gorgeous cinematography bring to life Edwardian England's rural and urban sides.

The Madness of King George, 1994.

Directed by Nicolas Hytner. George III had the unfortunate distinction of being the king who lost the American colonies. Although portrayed as a devil by radicals of the time (the French and American revolutions had every intellectual's mind on democracy), he was one of the most emotionally stable of kings. It was great irony, then, that he was plagued for the last thirty years of his life with a disease that causes dementia. This movie covers his first bout with the frightening illness, during which time his foppish eldest son does his best to seize the throne. Stars Nigel Hawthorne, Helen Mirren, and Ian Holm.

Chapter 4
Your Ancestors Were Immigrants

So it's pack up your sea-stores, consider no longer!
Ten dollars a week isn't very bad pay,
With no taxes or tithes to devour up your wages,
At home on the green fields of Amerikay.

Since European explorers first started exploring the North American continent, it has been considered the land of opportunity. It was a New World, lush with forests and rivers. It offered a sanctuary, a new beginning far from over-developed, overpopulated Europe.

The first people to come to North America arrived so many thousands of years ago that they are thought of as indigenous to this continent. The ethnic groups known today as Native Americans came not from Europe but from Asia. The ocean's level was lower then, so they were able to make the arduous, freezing journey on foot over a "land bridge" from what is now northeastern Russia to Alaska. They traveled here through centuries, spreading east and south to populate the plains, forests, hills, and mountains of what would become the Americas and Canada.

Who was next to arrive is a matter of some conjecture. Every American schoolchild learns about the voyages of Christopher Columbus beginning in 1492. Probably a few centuries before that, both Icelandic Vikings and missionaries from Ireland had stopped along America's east coast. Even if he was not the first European to arrive, Columbus was the first to arouse public fervor about the New World. Up to that time its existence to the European mind had been little more than myth. Once Spain expressed a political interest in claiming some of this vast new land,

Early colonists came into contact with Native American peoples. Here, a messenger from the Narragansett people is shown arranging a peaceful treaty with William Bradford, governor of the Plymouth Colony.

European nations became eager to annex a piece of America. By the early 1600s England had established itself as the trade leader in a very valuable commodity from America's Southeast. The indigenous peoples of that area taught the British farmers to grow—and use—tobacco. Pipe smoking quickly became an obsession all over Europe. Some smokers in England were even inspired to poetry.

> Tobacco is an Indian weed
> Grows green in the morn, cut down at eve.
> It shows our decay, that we are but clay.
> Think of this when you're smoking tobacco.
>
> The ashes that are left behind
> Do serve to put us all in mind
> That unto dust return we must.
> Think of this when you're smoking tobacco.

The majority of Americans have at least one family line that can be traced to Britain. Many of those original immigrant ancestors date from the seventeenth century, when the

Quakers were among the Nonconformist religious groups who fled England for America. The Quakers were led by William Penn.

English crown began encouraging entrepreneurs to set up trade settlements in America. The London Company sent a group of people to colonize Virginia tobacco country in 1607. Their settlement was called Jamestown, after King James I. Soon the Northeast and Canada were also being settled by Britons. By 1650, 20,000 Englishmen had come to the Massachusetts Bay Colony and spread into Rhode Island, New Hampshire, and Connecticut.

Surely the most famous seventeenth-century British immigrants to America were the Pilgrims who sailed on the *Mayflower*, landing at Plymouth Rock in 1620. Although only fifty of them survived their first winter in the New World, they set an inspiring precedent. These people were Puritans in a land with an official religion that they found too materialistic. Those who did not agree with the king's Church of England were known as Nonconformists or Separatists and were persecuted in Britain. From the time of the Pilgrims' courageous voyage to America in the name of religious freedom, the New World came to represent a haven for the rights of individuals. This credo was still central in the late eighteenth century, when the men who drafted the Declaration of Independence of the United States of America listed our inalienable rights: life, liberty, and the pursuit of happiness.

Another important shipload of Nonconformists arrived in 1680: Quakers, led by William Penn. Penn's vision was to establish a colony where Quakers could hold meetings freely and engage in a life of commerce and community directed by their values of humility and friendship. Had the then King of England, Charles II, allowed it, Penn would have called his settlement New Wales in memory of his ancestors' homeland. Instead it became the city of Philadelphia, still a center for the Religious Society of Friends.

Adventurers and Convicts

Once the American colonies were founded in the seventeenth century, the British government did all it could to get people to move there. It was no easy task to keep the colonies livable and economically viable. The British government needed labor to work the fields and build roads, towns, and schools. It also needed educated people to run the businesses there.

There were always adventurers willing to go to America. Some of them were risk-taking entrepreneurs determined to make a fortune in the New World. Some were the roguish sons of landed gentry or wealthy merchants, who had annoyed their fathers to the point of being disowned as heirs. The younger sons of noblemen were also prime candidates for a new life in America. Only the eldest son stood to inherit land and property, so the younger sons might as well start anew across the Atlantic. Many women ended up in America because they married one of these adventurers. The daughter of a wealthy Englishman might be sent across to marry a successful businessman in the colonies.

These educated people made up the administrative core of

This 1855 Ford Madox Brown painting, entitled "The Last of England," captures the fortitude of the English emigrants.

the American Colonies. They ran the businesses, taught, and worked in government or as military officers. The colonies were still in need of hundreds of thousands of laborers to pave the way, literally, for a growing America. The British government turned to a source that could provide an endless stream of able-bodied young men: the prisons.

> My name is Jamie Raeburn, in Glasgow I was born.
> My place of habitation I'm forced to leave with scorn.
> From my place of habitation now I must go awa',
> Far from the bonnie hills and dales of Caledonia.

> It was early on one morning, just at the break of day,
> The turn-key he came up to us, and unto us did say,
> "Arise, you hapless convicts, arise you one and all!
> This is the day you are to stray from Caledonia."

Scottish convicts were among the first to be shipped to America. They were sent in the 1690s to work as free labor on two plantations started by Scotsmen in South Carolina. Not all of the convicts were hardened criminals. The justice system in Britain at that time made little difference in the punishment for murder and for shoplifting. That punishment was usually hanging. Being forced to work in America was actually a reprieve for the condemned.

One of the most common crimes was poaching or hunting on private lands. If a person were to hunt enough to make a living at it, it was hard not to trespass since all the good hunting grounds were purposely made the private property of noblemen. Many more of the convicts sent over were prisoners of war, including Scots and Welshmen who were caught standing up for their independence.

The system of forcing prisoners into American labor gangs was very successful. The British government sent over about 50,000 convicts from England alone between 1717 and 1775. They followed the same procedure when they began to colonize Australia.

Some of the prisoners sent to America were desperate to get back home. They served their time on the work gang—perhaps seven years, perhaps twenty-one—then caught the next boat back to Liverpool as soon as they were freed. Others, however, took this forced displacement as an opportunity to begin anew, leaving their checkered past behind. Many worked hard and were loyal to their "masters" on the plantation. When they completed the end of their sentence they were promoted to office manager or other responsible positions. Some became quite prosperous.

It is interesting to note that most of the people who came to America from the British Isles in the late seventeenth and early eighteenth centuries came voluntarily.

In the Middle Ages, all of Europe was under the feudal system, whereby a few people owned property and the rest were under their power. A person sold himself into servitude to one of these landowners. Both parties signed a contract, and the "indentured" servant agreed to work for his master

Settlers' wives and children often joined them after they were established in America. Here, the wives of the settlers of Jamestown arrive to meet their spouses.

for a specified number of years (usually decades). In return, he received certain minimum care for his family and a small plot of ground to farm.

This same system was set up in the American colonies, and tens of thousands of poor families sold themselves into a future of backbreaking work in a strange land—with one important difference, however. In medieval Europe, indentured servants had no hope. They had to become servants just to survive from day to day, and their children could expect to do the same. But those British people who became indentured laborers in America were coming to the land of opportunity.

There was no established aristocracy, and every individual had a chance to make something of himself or herself by hard work, cleverness, strength, and courage. Also, a vast area of land lay undeveloped. An indentured couple in America were laborers on a plantation or farm for four to ten years and then were able to establish their own farmstead or small business. Most important, they knew they were making a better future available to their children. The generations that sprang from the poor Britons who emigrated here still survive in modern America.

Across the Raging Main

It is not an easy decision for people to leave their native land. Throughout history, whenever a mass exodus from Britain has been necessary for economic or religious reasons, those bold enough to consider the move have had to weigh the consequences carefully.

The voyage across the Atlantic took anywhere from six to twelve weeks in the eighteenth century. There were no steamships, only wooden vessels with sails. Shipwrecks were common. Passengers were packed into the hold of the ship like livestock. Frequently they ran out of food a week before landing. Dysentery and other highly communicable diseases claimed the lives of perhaps a quarter of those who attempted the voyage. Once they landed, the indentured immigrants faced the ordeal of being sold like slaves. Starvation and freezing were threats in the northeastern winters, while the southern colonies were plagued with malaria in the summertime. For all this "opportunity," a man might well pay a year's wages to the shipping company.

Yet people continued to come. For most of Britain during this period, life was at a level of unbearable poverty. It was better to try a new, difficult avenue than to stay on the road to certain misery. In Scotland, civil war and frequent changes in administration left people homeless, jobless, or running for their lives from whatever new regime was in power. Poverty was especially bad in Scotland. Although England was expanding its hold there, agriculture could not sustain the growing population. Even nobility lived in squalor. Until the mid-eighteenth century when new technology was developed to drain and fertilize the soggy Scottish soil properly, starvation forced countless people to seek a better lot in America.

Although many thousands of families found a new life in

the New World, some still longed for the homeland that had
forsaken them.

> Hame [*home*], hame, hame;
> hame I'd like to be;
> Hame, hame, hame
> In my ain country.
> Where the wild deer run
> In the glen I'll never see.
> Sure my heart will aye remain
> In my ain country.

Land of Liberty

By the middle of the eighteenth century, America was on its
way to independence from Britain. The "patriots" who led
the American Revolutionary War were seen as heroes by
radicals in England, Scotland, and Wales. The buildup to
the French Revolution in the same decades provided further
inspiration to Nonconformists in Britain. A prolonged stay in
either France or America became a necessary part of training
to be a free thinker. Some of those students of democracy
thought Britain was too far gone to save, and they chose to
stay in America. Political and religious nonconformity went
hand in hand. The Church of England and King George III
became the prime public enemies, standing in the way of
religious freedom and democracy. The burgeoning egalitarian states of America and France were thought of as models
and potential saviors.

> And when upon the British shore
> The thundering guns of France shall roar,
> Vile George shall trembling stand
> Or flee his native land.

A fervent pride of heritage accompanied this movement
away from British establishment. Even ancient Celtic
druidism made a comeback in Wales at the beginning of the
nineteenth century. Unitarianism, a Christian denomination
that questioned the doctrine that Jesus was actually God's

son, became popular among Welsh radicals. Many such "heretical" Nonconformists as these had to flee to safety in Holland or America.

Scottish Nonconformists had been making similar flights to America for over 100 years. Since the mid-seventeenth century radicals had been trying to keep Scotland an independent country, or at least a self-governing part of Britain. Frequent changes in the British monarchy meant sudden changes in "official" opinion. Each time this happened, a new group of freethinkers was rounded up and deported to America, and even more fled there on their own. Despite their remarkable courage in battle, the Scots were outclassed by the modern weapons and training of the British military. Each defeat meant that another ship packed with Scottish prisoners of war would head for the New World.

In 1776 the Declaration of Independence of the United States of America was signed, and the new government got to work on a constitution. The central premise was to respect each human equally and to give every individual a chance for personal success. This philosophy is still the magnet that draws foreigners to the shores of the United States.

Once independence was achieved, Britain could no longer shunt off its criminals to the New World, nor were merchants sponsored to represent the Crown's interest in the colonies. It happened, however, that massive changes were in store for Europe, changes that would push hundreds of thousands more Britons to make the journey to the United States. The turn into the nineteenth century was the dawn of the Industrial Revolution.

New technologies, catapulted forward by the development of the steam engine, changed the workplace in the Western hemisphere. Factories sprang up in London, Manchester, Glasgow, Cardiff, and dozens of other cities. Everyone crammed into these cities to get a piece of the action. Rich company owners exploited their uneducated workers, turning a deaf ear to the horrors of sweatshops and child labor. The result was overpopulation, unsanitary conditions, crime, and homelessness. Slums developed around the fringes of urban centers. It was a demoralizing, filthy lifestyle, no better than that of the indentured servants of the Middle Ages.

Again the land of opportunity beckoned. Although U.S. cities were experiencing similar uncontrolled growth, there remained vast areas of undisturbed nature, untapped resources. Every worker who could afford it got on a boat to the United States. Many men went alone because they didn't have the money to take along their families. Some joined the British navy as a way to make a salary while getting out of their stifling homelands.

Ideally, a man would find work and earn money quickly, and soon he could pay the passage for his wife and children. The reality was much different. Many letters were lost between the United States and Britain, and just as many hearts were lost to new sweethearts once couples were parted by the Atlantic. Nevertheless, an escape to the United States was every working woman's dream:

> Come all you fair and tender maidens,
> Don't slight your sailors whilst they're at sea,
> For they'll come home, they'll make you their own,
> And they'll bring you over to Amerikay.

Give Me Your Poor . . .

By the early nineteenth century the steamship had replaced the sailing vessel as the mode of transit from Britain to the United States. The city of Liverpool, England, was by far the most important point of embarkation. People traveled from all over Britain to board an U.S.-bound ship in Liverpool. By the end of the nineteenth century, the port had become a transfer point for emigrants traveling to America from other parts of Europe and Asia.

Many competing shipping lines operated out of Liverpool's harbor. Some were fly-by-night or ill-conceived ventures that ended in tragedy at sea. Others became well established and handled transport to points on America's east coast for half a century or more. All of them demanded

Castle Garden, a converted amusement park in New York, was the port of entry for many of the nineteenth century's British emigrants.

payment in advance from passengers. Even in steamships, conditions for traveling across the Atlantic were still more suitable for cattle than for humans. In 1848, of the 106,000 Scots and Irish who emigrated, over 12,000 died at sea. Another 7,000 were so ill when they landed that they didn't survive more than a few weeks in their new country.

The most prominent symbol of the United States' welcoming policy toward immigrants is the Statue of Liberty in New York City. Next to it lies Ellis Island, the most famous port of entry in the United States. If you are studying Polish immigration, or even Irish, these icons of American freedom will figure as an important part of your ancestors' past. This is not the case with the majority of British family lines in the United States. Ellis Island was not established as a port of entry until 1892, and most British immigrants had arrived in the United States by then.

Nevertheless, it is still fascinating to learn about Ellis Island. Because its heyday was in the early twentieth century, the arrival of immigrants there is well documented in records, photographs, and even moving images. You can get a clear sense of what immigration was like. In 1924 Ellis was shut down as a port, and it fell into disrepair. It was reopened in 1990 as a beautiful museum, a homage to the 12 million courageous people who passed through this gateway to the land of opportunity.

Many of the British who arrived in New York in the nine-

Many English and Scottish emigrants entered the United States through Baltimore's Fort McHenry.

teenth century came to the predecessor of Ellis Island, a converted amusement park called Castle Garden. Not every British immigrant landed in New York, however. Baltimore's Fort McHenry harbor drew thousands of unskilled laborers from England and Scotland. There was always work to be had in Baltimore if you had some muscle. And a certain Mrs. Koether kept a boarding house where you could stay until you found your way. For fifty years she fed and housed about 40,000 newly arrived laborers per year, and was paid about seventy-five cents per day for each boarder.

British kinship ties to the United States were strong; they had been growing since the seventeenth century. Many people who came from a certain area of Britain would head directly for a town in the United States populated by immigrants from the same region. Ethnic districts developed in most cities, where people of similar heritage could feel less alone in a new land.

A striking example was the state of Pennsylvania. In the nineteenth century people from Wales flooded that state to join and expand Welsh communities established in the late 1600s. Welsh immigrants were usually factory or mine workers seeking better pay or a cleaner environment for their children. They had valuable machine skills that were highly

marketable as the United States pushed to develop westward. William Penn's Philadelphia soon overflowed into the
surrounding countryside, given the Welsh name Merion.
Almost every place-name in that region—Radnor, Bryn
Mawr, Narberth, to name a few—is a reminder of the swell-
ing ranks of prosperous Welsh immigrants in the eighteenth
and nineteenth centuries.

Of course, not everyone stayed on the east coast. The
U.S. government wanted to expand to the west. It encour-
aged people to stake out land in every direction: Texas,
Wisconsin, even California. This was much the same strat-
egy that the British government had used when it encour-
aged entrepreneurs to brave the wilderness of the New
World in the early seventeenth century. Some British
American families toughed it out as pioneers, claiming farm-
land in the west. Many hardy young men just over from
England or Scotland tried their hands as cowherds in
Kansas, lumberjacks in northern Michigan, or gold prospec-
tors in California.

Families moved around within states and all over the
growing American nation. They met other new arrivals from
other countries and learned new customs and ways of view-
ing the world. Those families that had been in America since
colonial times had already begun to develop a distinctive
British American culture. It was influenced by the traditional
heritage of England, Scotland, and Wales but adapted to fit
the free-spirited melting pot called the United States of
America.

As you begin to piece together your family history, make
yourself a timeline showing which of your ancestors was
where, when. Then superimpose that over a history timeline.
How many of your family lines were in America when the
Declaration of Independence was signed? What were your
ancestors doing during the War of 1812 or the Civil War?
How did new technology, such as passenger trains spanning
the American continent, affect the movement of your
family? Suddenly facts that can look pretty boring in a social
studies textbook spring to life because they have to do with
you.

George Northrup, a Minnesota gold miner, was among many British settlers who represented the move westward.

Resources

PORTS OF ENTRY

Stern, Gail, ed. *Freedom's Doors: Immigrant Ports of Entry to the United States.* **Philadelphia: Balch Institute Press, 1986.**

Meant to accompany an exhibit about immigration, this book is informative and full of photos of interesting artifacts and documents.

Stolarik, M. Mark, ed. *Forgotten Doors: The Other Ports of Entry to the United States.* **Philadelphia: Balch Institute Press, 1988.**

We all know about Ellis Island. This book discusses the importance of other processing stations, such as Cape May of Philadelphia and Fort McHenry of Baltimore, earlier ports worked by many Liverpool shipping lines. Port of Boston, Port of New Orleans, and a few west coast harbors are also covered.

AMERICA DURING THE COLONIAL PERIOD

Avi. *The Fighting Ground.* **New York: Lippincott, 1984.**

The fictional story of a teenage boy who joins the army to fight in the American Revolution, only to find that his most important struggle is in his own growing self.

Cappos, Lester J. *Atlas of Early American History. Revolutionary Era 1760–1790.* **Princeton: Princeton University Press, 1976.**

This atlas shows streets, towns, and hillsides where battles took place, along with important historical places in the

American colonies. It is accompanied by brief descriptions of the battles.

Faragher, John Mack. *The Encyclopedia of Colonial and Revolutionary America.* **New York: Facts on File, 1990.**

Listed alphabetically and accompanied by illustrations and maps, the entries in this encyclopedia include everything from the names of the first colonies to the names of the "founding fathers." It's a good resource to have handy if you're looking at British American documents from the eighteenth century.

Grimer, Roberta. *My Thomas: A Novel of Martha Jefferson's Life.* **New York: Doubleday, 1993.**

Using biographical and historical facts, this is a fictionalization of Thomas Jefferson's lifetime told through the eyes of his wife. Includes factual genealogical tables on the Jeffersons.

O'Toole, Dennis A., and Strick, Lisa W. *In the Minds and Hearts of the People: Five Amercian Patriots and the Road to Revolution.* **Washington, DC: National Portrait Gallery, 1974.**

Celebrates the lives and contributions of patriots Jared Ingersol, Landon Carter, Christopher Gadsden, John Lamb, and Josiah Quincy, Jr. Illustrated with paintings from the Gallery's collection.

Rappaport, Doreen. *The Boston Coffee Party.* **New York: Harper & Row, 1988.**

A novel about two young sisters who help with a plot to overthrow some shifty merchants in colonial Boston.

1776 Relived: See and Visit the American Revolution. **Maplewood, NJ: Hammond, 1974.**

Color maps and illustrations celebrating the American colonies' struggle for independence. Color photos of Revolutionary War sites as they appear today accompany text explaining the importance of each place.

Wolf, William J. *Benedict Arnold.* **Ashfield, MA: Paideia Publishing, 1990.**

A novelization of the life of early America's most famous traitor.

BRITISH AMERICAN LIFE AND HISTORY

Bell, James P. *Our Quaker Friends of Ye Olden Time.* **Conway, AR: Oldbuck Press, 1994.**

The antiquated title of this book reflects its 1902 origins. Includes photos and an index of 360 Quaker surnames. This is not an exhaustive list of Quakers in the United States, but it does have some interesting text about traditions and customs.

Cornelius, James M. *The English Americans.* **New York: Chelsea House, 1990.**

A short introduction for young people to the unique contributions that English settlers have made to American culture. The book describes their reasons for leaving their home country, their passage over, where they settled, and how they adapted in America.

Cutrer, Thomas W. *The English Texans.* **San Antonio: University of Texas, 1985.**

The story of English and Welsh Americans who moved to the biggest state to make a life for themselves. Most of these were young men who arrived in the United States in the mid-nineteenth century and couldn't find work in the eastern cities.

Dublin, Thomas. *Transforming Women's Work: New England Lives in the Industrial Revolution.* **Ithaca: Cornell University Press, 1994.**

The Age of Machinery changed everyone's lives with the rapid development of new technologies. In some ways the new working world affected women more than men. It opened new opportunities for them to contribute to their community's economic base, yet it also made them prey to unfair labor practices that are still a problem for today's immigrant women.

Faragher, John Mack, ed. *The Encyclopedia of Colonial and Revolutionary America.* **New York: Facts on File, 1990.**

A concise source for information on the period from 1600 to 1783 in America and Canada.

Greene, Jack P. *Pursuits of Happiness.* **Chapel Hill: University of North Carolina Press, 1988.**

Explores the social development of the early British colonies and how British customs influenced the growth of American culture. British immigrants helped to decide everything from the way we celebrate Christmas to the way we build houses.

Hinshaw, William Wade. *Encyclopedia of American Quaker Genealogy.* **Baltimore: Genealogical Publishing, 1991.**

This resource depends on thousands of documents reaching back to the seventeenth century. You can look up your surname and be cross-referenced to other family lines connected by marriage.

Olson, Lee. *Marmalade and Whiskey; British Remittance Men in the West.* **Golden, CO: Fulcrum, 1993.**

Learn about the daily life and transplanted traditions of upper-class Englishmen who moved to western regions of America. There were small communities of these young noblemen, usually second sons of landed gentry who were not entitled to inherit.

Rasmussen, Louis J. *Railway Passenger Lists of Overland Trains to San Francisco and the West.* **Colma, CA: San Francisco Historic Records, 1966.**

This directory is a great piece of scholarship, covering internal immigration within the United States during the years 1870 and 1890. Often in a genealogical search it is a family's big move west that is one of the most elusive periods to track. Especially valuable because it is indexed by passenger name.

Whicker, Alan. *Whicker's New World: America Through the Eyes and Lives of Resident Brits.* Lon-don: **Weidenfeld and Nicolson, 1985.**

A personal and humorous journey through English America, illustrated with moving photographs by Valerie Kleeman. You can hear in the words of these recent immigrants the delight, enchantment, and horror at what they observed in their new home. Some didn't find it all that different from England.

Woods, L. Milton. *British Gentlemen in the Wild West: The Era of the Intensely English Cowboy.* **New York: Free Press/Collier Macmillan, 1989.**

Not all English immigrants settled in New England. Not all cowboys were illiterate roughnecks. Here is a fascinat-ing look at some educated Englishmen who left their native home for a life of adventure in the American West.

SCOTTISH AMERICAN LIFE AND HISTORY

Adams, Ian H., and Somerville, Meredyth. *Cargoes of Despair and Hope: Scottish Emigration to North America, 1603–1803.* **Edinburgh: J. Donald, 1993.**

Immigration from Scotland to America took place in waves, reflecting difficult circumstances in the old coun-try. This book explains those circumstances and the dis-crepancies between what the Scots expected and what was actually waiting in the New World.

Landsman, Ned C. *Scotland and Its First American Colony, 1683–1765.* **Princeton: Princeton University Press, 1985.**

The first Scots to form their own colony in the New World settled in New Jersey. This history considers the reasons for their coming and aspects of their new life. It contrasts their colony with predominantly British settlements, such as Massachussetts.

Lehmann, William C. *Scottish and Scotch-Irish Con-tributions to Early American Life and Culture.* **Port**

Washington, NY: National University Publications, 1978.

Considers the lifestyles of Scottish Americans both in the colonial period and the nineteenth century, and how these immigrants influenced the formation of American traditions. Their influence can be felt in politics, literature, and farming techniques, for example.

Sher, Richard B., and Smitten, Jeffrey R. *Scotland and America in the Age of Enlightenment.* **Edinburgh: Edinburgh University Press, 1990.**

While the American colonies were organizing and fighting for independence, a major intellectual revolution was happening in Europe. Not only was America influenced by this revolution, but many believe that the movement toward independence was a result of it.

WELSH AMERICAN LIFE AND HISTORY

Ashton, Elwyn T. *The Welsh in the United States.* **Hove, Sussex, England: Caldra House, 1984.**

A brief overview of Welsh American history, from William Penn's establishment of Philadelphia through the late nineteenth century, when mine shutdowns in Wales drove laborers to seek a new life.

Jones, William D. *Wales in America: Scranton and the Welsh, 1860–1920.* **Cardiff: University of Wales Press, 1993.**

A history of emigration of Welsh to Scranton, Pennsylvania, and their contribution to American society. Includes a description of the settlements, farming, intellectual life (there were several Welsh-language newspapers), and religion.

Williams, Jay G. *Memory Stones: A History of Welsh-Americans in Central New York and Their Churches.* **Fleischmanns, NY: Purple Mountain Press, 1993.**

The Welsh emigrants to America played a key role in the development of the Protestant church in the Northeast.

This book traces how that religious foundation was built upon in the nineteenth century.

EMIGRATION TO AMERICA

From England or Great Britain

Allan, Morton. *A Directory of European Passenger Steamship Arrivals.* **Baltimore: Genealogical Publishing, 1980.**

You can look up ships by name of vessel, date of arrival, and ship company. It does not include a passenger list, but the information can help you determine which lists to check.

Berthoff, Rowland. *British Immigrants in Industrial America, 1790–1950.* **Cambridge, MA: Harvard University Press, 1953.**

This history considers what caused British workers to leave their own industrialized land and come to the new cities of America. Many of them had been laid off from their factory or mining jobs. In America they found opportunities to use their skills in developing urban areas.

Boyer, Carl. *Ancestral Lines Revised: 190 Families in England, Wales, Germany, New England, New York, New Jersey, and Pennsylvania.* **Newhall, CA: C. Boyer, 1981.**

An interesting combined treatment of family lines from Britain and Germany and how they manifested themselves on the northeast coast of the United States.

Coldham, Peter Wilson. *English Adventurers and Emigrants, 1609–1660.* **Baltimore: Genealogical Publishing, 1984.**

———. *English Adventurers and Emigrants, 1661–1733.* **Baltimore: Genealogical Publishing, 1985.**

These two volumes were compiled from records of the High Court of Admiralty. Those court documents have nothing directly to do with genealogy, but family historians long ago discovered that the records contain information that may not be found elsewhere, such as birth registers from very early immigrants to America and Canada.

Erickson, Charlotte. *Invisible Immigrants*. Ithaca, NY: Cornell University Press, 1990.

An examination of how English and Scottish immigrants adapted once they arrived and settled in America. Uses nineteenth-century sources to chart the troubles faced in the New World, as well as the unlimited power the immigrants felt over the indigenous peoples.

Filby, P. William. *Passenger and Immigration List Index*. Detroit: Gale Research, 1981.

A guide to published records of immigration to America. This is a basic book for all genealogists; it is especially strong on British immigration and east-coast ports of entry.

Hoff, Henry B. *English Origins of American Colonists*. Baltimore: Genealogical Publishing, 1991.

Excerpts from wills and other documents from the seventeenth and eighteenth centuries are used to give a personal side of immigration and life in the New World. Each entry is accompanied by notes explaining its significance to early American history.

Johnson, Lorand Victor. *Is This Your English Ancestor?* Shaker Heights, OH: L.V. Johnson, 1979.

This is a directory of the names and locations of 13,000 Quakers who were banished from Great Britain and Ireland and sought relief from religious persecution in America. If you have Quaker roots in England, you may find your surname here.

Kaminkow, Jack, and Kaminkow, Marion J. *A List of Emigrants from England to America, 1718–1759*. Baltimore: Magna Carta, 1981.

Traces movements during the colonial period, including immigration patterns to and from the British West Indies.

Knoff, Dorothy C., and Knoff, Gerald E. *Thirty-one English Emigrants Who Came to New England by 1662.* Bath, England: Gateway, 1989.

This directory follows the descendants of thirty-one families who were among the first to arrive in America from England. It offers valuable shortcuts to family historians by listing vital information on seventeenth-century family members. Organized by surname.

Lancour, Harold. *A Bibliography of Ship Passenger Lists, 1583–1825.* New York: New York Public Library, 1963.

If you can't find the right passenger list in the National Archives, this book might help you locate it. It is organized by port of entry and period of immigration.

The Norman People and Their Existing Descendants in the British Dominions and the United States of America. Baltimore: Genealogical Publishing, 1989.

British names such as De Burgh and De Valera date back to the nobility established after the Norman conquest in the eleventh century. Trace the movement of your Norman family name. Originally published in 1874.

Roberts, Gary Boyd. *English Origins of New England Families.* Baltimore: Genealogical Publishing, 1985.

A thorough lineage of families with British roots, using the New England historical and genealogical register.

Scott, Kenneth. *British Aliens in the United States During the War of 1812.* Baltimore: Genealogical Publishing, 1979.

Scott has compiled the names of British citizens who fought or worked on American soil in the early nineteenth century. Such people can be difficult to trace because they may have stayed here only briefly and not applied for American citizenship. Some, however, ended up marrying (or at least having children with) Americans.

Seventeenth Century Immigration to North America from Great Britain and Ireland. Salt Lake City:

Genealogical Department of The Church of Jesus Christ of Latter-day Saints, 1977.

Quick and clear, this twenty-four-page introduction is a great place to start learning how to use LDS resources (which means almost all important resources) if your ancestors came to America during the precolonial and early colonial periods.

Smith, Clifford Neal. *British and German Deserters, Dischargees, and Prisoners of War Who May Have Remained in Canada and the United States, 1774–1783.* McNeal, AR: Westland Publications, 1988.

There are plenty of resources for finding records of ancestors in the British Army. This book is useful because it traces the settlement patterns of some of those troops after the point to which they're traced in Army records.

———. *British Deportees to America.* Dekalb, IL: Westland Publications, 1974.

This is an impressive eight-volume resource cataloguing British who were exiled from their homeland between the years 1760 and 1775. A cumulative index helps you find your ancestor by surname.

Thompson, Roger. *Mobility and Migration.* Amherst: University of Massachusetts Press, 1994.

During the seventeenth century, immigrants from East Anglia (southeast England) were among the first to settle America's New England. This history tells what prompted them to leave home and what they found in the New World.

Weaver, Jack W. and Lester, DeeGee. *Immigrants from Great Britain and Ireland.* Westport, CT: Greenwood Press, 1986.

A directory of archival material in the United States and Canada, with instructions on which sources to use for your particular search.

From Scotland

Beckett, J. D. *A Dictionary of Scottish Emigrants into England and Wales.* Manchester, England: Anglo-Scottish Family History Society, 1989.

Family research can be a little confusing when your ancestors moved around before coming to America. This book
may help if any of your Scottish kin moved to England or
Wales at some point.

**Dobson, David. *Directory of Scots Banished to the
American Plantations, 1650–1775*. Baltimore: Genealogical Publishing, 1983.**

Scottish citizens accused of everything from illegal hunting to treason were exiled. Look in this listing to see if your
ancestors were thought to be shady characters by the
Kingdom of Scotland.

**———. *Directory of Scots in the Carolinas, 1680–1830*.
Baltimore: Genealogical Publishing, 1986.**

This guide concentrates on what happened to Scottish
families once they had settled on the southeast coast of
America. Organized by surname, each entry gives a concise account of the settlement of the family.

**———. *The Original Scots Colonists of Early America,
1612–1783*. Baltimore: Genealogical Publishing, 1989.**

The first Scots to settle across the Atlantic are listed,
accompanied by explanations for their emigration and
discussion of lifestyle in the New World. Some of these
people were merchants and settled in Massachussetts Bay
Colony; others were convicts who went to labor in the
Southern plantations. Includes index of surnames.

**———. *Scots on the Chesapeake, 1607–1830*. Balti-
more: Genealogical Publishing, 1992.**

A directory of Scottish families who settled in Maryland
and Virginia. Each entry, alphabetized by surname, includes landing date, port of entry, and where the family
settled.

**———. *Scottish-American Court Records, 1733–1783*.
Baltimore: Genealogical Publishing, 1991.**

The author explains these important genealogical documents and offers his findings in a concise form. Court

records give evidence of names, relationships, property rights, and other information. Includes indexes to the court records.

Donaldson, Gordon. *The Scots Overseas.* **London: T. Nelson, 1966.**

This book is particularly useful to genealogists for its good bibliographies at the end of each chapter. Deals with emigration to America, Canada, the West Indies, and other British colonies.

Durning, William P. *The Scotch-Irish.* **La Mesa, CA: Irish Family Names Society, 1991.**

The Scotch Irish are those who emigrated from Scotland to Northern Ireland. They were either lured or sent there by the King of England, who was trying to lay a solid English claim in the province of Ulster. Many of those families subsequently moved to Canada and the United States.

Meyer, Duane. *The Highland Scots of North Carolina, 1732–1766.* **Chapel Hill: University of North Carolina Press, 1961.**

This is both a history and a catalog of northern Scottish emigrants who made their way to the plantation country of North Carolina. These were years of prosperity for Scottish Americans; by then strong networks had been established across the Atlantic to absorb new immigrants into communities.

Scottish-American Genealogist. **Harbor City, CA: Hartwell.**

An annual periodical featuring essays, a letter forum, and updates on genealogical resources in America and Scotland.

Smith, Abbot E. *Colonists in Bondage.* **Chapel Hill: University of North Carolina Press, 1947.**

This book explains the waves of convicts sent to the New World in the seventeenth and eighteenth centuries, taking into account political changes in Scotland and other influential factors. The history includes the landing place of the convicts and what became of them in America.

Whyte, Donald. *A Dictionary of Scottish Emigrants to Canada Before Confederation.* **Toronto: Ontario Genealogical Society, 1986.**

A valuable source interpreting Scottish and Canadian emigration and immigration registers for the eighteenth and nineteenth centuries. Surnames are listed alphabetically and include date and port of entry.

————. *A Dictionary of Scottish Emigrants to the U.S.A.* **Baltimore: Magna Carta, 1986.**

This two-volume set includes thousands of surnames. It was compiled from passenger lists, land deeds, wills, and other documents. Appendix includes research tools such as bibliographies and a cross-referenced index.

Wicklein, Edward C. *The Scots of Vernon and Adjacent Townships, Waukesha County, Wisconsin.* **Big Bend, WI: E. C. Wicklein, 1974.**

A sampling of Scots who braved the cold and forests to make a life in the Northern Midwest. It includes details on exactly which families came to this area and substantiates its claims with vital records and other documents.

From Wales

Blackwell, Henry. *A Bibliography of Welsh Americana.* **Aberystwyth, Wales: National Library of Wales, 1977.**

A list of sources both in Wales and the United States, Welsh American publications, and published family histories.

Davies, Phillips G. *The Welsh in Wisconsin.* **Madison: State Historical Society of Wisconsin, 1982.**

Seeking opportunities and cheap land in the nineteenth century, many Welsh families in the United States ventured to the wooded northern Midwest. This book gives a detailed description of who came, where they settled, and how they made a living.

Holt, Constance Wall. *Welsh Women.* **Metuchen, NJ: Scarecrow Press, 1993.**

An annotated bibliography of Welsh and Welsh American women. It covers books and articles about their family life, work, literacy and education, and the hardships and freedoms they experienced on either side of the Atlantic.

Jones, Alexander. *The Cymry of '76, or, Welshmen and Their Descendants of the American Revolution.* **Baltimore: Clearfield Co., 1989.**

Transcripion of an address given in 1855, celebrating the Welsh contribution to American independence. Besides providing a valuable sense of Welsh American pride in the colonial period, it also names battles and events in which Welsh regiments participated.

Thomas, Robert David. *Hanes Cymry America (A History of the Welsh in America).* **Translated by Phillips G. Davies. Lanham, MD: University Press of America, 1983.**

English translation of an important 1872 book of Welsh American family histories. Entries include some valuable information about family movements and individual characters hard to find elsewhere.

LANGUAGES

Betts, Clive. *Culture in Crisis: The Future of the Welsh Language.* **Upton, U.K.: Ffynnon Press, 1976.**

As part of the United Kingdom, whose official language is English, Wales has not found it easy to preserve its language and traditions. This story has a happy ending, though, because it tells of the revival in teaching and use of Welsh.

Davies, Dewi. *Welsh Place-Names and Their Meanings.* **Brecon, Wales: D. Davies, 1977.**

Many of the most important Welsh words for a family historian to learn are those contained in place-names. They give a sense of history, as well as offering some vital clues about the area's past.

James, Dan Lynn. *Cwrs Cymraeg Llafar: Conversational Welsh Course.* **Llandybie, Wales: C. Davies, 1975.**

A two-volume series of lessons in practical Welsh, including grammar, vocabulary, pronunciation, and useful phrases.

Latham, Ronald Edward. *Revised Medieval Latin Word-List from British and Irish Sources.* **London: Oxford University Press, 1965.**

With this word list you don't need to fear early legal documents from England. Latham sifted through thousands of documents and made a glossary of all the Latin words he found in "legalese" from before the sixteenth century.

MacThomais, Ruaraidh. *Gaelic Learner's Handbook.* **Glasgow: Gairm Publications, 1973.**

Text in both English and Gaelic. Includes a glossary of terms, phrases, and sentences conveniently arranged by subject, along with a pronunciation guide. This approach is designed for acquiring a cursory knowledge of the language—enough to read street signs and communicate with shopkeepers in the west of Wales.

Martin, Charles Trice. *The Record Interpreter.* **Chichester, England: Phillimore, 1982.**

A collection of abbreviations, Latin words, and names used in early English manuscripts and records. The inclusion of abbreviations is particularly helpful to the novice.

Rycraft, Ann. *English Mediaeval Handwriting.* **York, England: University of York Borthwick Institute of Historical Research, 1973.**

A good lesson in deciphering old documents. The author

uses specific examples from visual aids (twelve facsimiles of early legal papers and registers) to show how to recognize letters of the alphabet that have changed significantly over the centuries.

Thomson, Derick S. *The Companion to Gaelic Scotland.* **Oxford: Blackwell, 1983.**

An encyclopedia of places in the Scottish highlands where Gaelic is still the primary language. You can look up a place-name where you had an ancestor and find out whether you will run into a lot of Gaelic in your search.

————. *The New English-Gaelic Dictionary.* **Glasgow: Gairm Publications, 1981.**

If you need to find out the meaning of one or two Welsh words in a document, sometimes a dictionary will suffice. This is a good one to check because of its fairly recent publication date (older dictionaries use out-of-date English to translate the Welsh).

IMMIGRANT SUCCESS STORIES

Mitchell, Broadus. *Alexander Hamilton.* **New York: Macmillan, 1962.**

Volume 1 covers this Scottish American "founding father's" early years, 1757–1788, and volume 2 follows his "National Adventure," 1788–1804. Hamilton has the distinction of being the only Scottish-born signer of the Declaration of Independence.

Penn, William. *The Papers of William Penn.* **Philadelphia: University of Pennsylvania Press, 1987.**

You may not want to read this five-volume set cover to cover, but it is interesting to see what this famous Welsh American had in mind as he developed the Society of Friends, the Quaker congregations of Philadelphia.

Silver, Charles. *Charles Chaplin, An Appreciation.* **New York: Museum of Modern Art, 1989.**

Published on the centenary of his birth, this color-illustrated book gives biographical information on the English American comic genius, as well as showing artworks that have been inspired by his motion pictures.

Swetnam, George. *Andrew Carnegie.* **Boston: Twayne Publishers, 1980.**

A biography of the steel magnate, the quintessential Scottish immigrant-who-made-good-in-America.

Wildes, Harry Emerson. *William Penn.* **New York: Macmillan, 1974.**

A biography of the courageous Quaker after whom Pennsylvania is named. Follows Penn through his boyhood in Wales, his religious and political leadership in England, and the fulfillment of his dream to establish a Quaker settlement in America.

MUSIC AND DANCE

Elliott, Kenneth, and Rimmer, Frederick. *A History of Scottish Music.* **London: BBC, 1988.**

A general overview of traditional Scottish folk music and other forms that have mingled with it over the centuries. These outside influences have included Southern English, Irish, and even French music traditions, and developments in classical and rock music.

Forrest, John. *Morris and Matachin.* **London: English Folk Dance and Song Society, 1984.**

Morris and Matachin are two styles of rural dance from the north of England, dating to the Middle Ages. Originally they were performed in costumes representing folk heroes such as Robin Hood. This is a history of the dance forms, including their musical origins and social significance.

Haun, Orvie, and Stompers, Stevens. *Introduction to Clogging. Intermediate Clogging. Advanced Clogging Steps.*

This is a three-volume video series teaching traditional English rhythm dance. It is performed in wooden-soled shoes, especially in the north of England. This series concentrates on the British American clogging tradition, centered in the Appalachians.

Kennedy, Peter, and Parfrey, Raymond. *Folksongs of Britain and Ireland.* **London: Cassell, 1975.**

A major opus, this book is over 800 pages long and includes songs in English, Scots Gaelic, Irish Gaelic, Manx Gaelic, Welsh, Cornish, and various gypsy languages. Melodies written out with guitar chords.

Lewish, Gareth H. "Welsh Choral Tradition, Fact and Myth," in *Welsh Music: Cerddoriaeth Cymrie,* **Vol. 5, No. 4, 1976–77, pp. 57–73.**

Nineteenth-century Welsh music making is discussed in its historical and social context. A fascinating aspect of this work is learning how the rise of Methodism in Wales affected the development of the now-famous Welsh style of choral singing.

———. *Travellers' Songs: From England and Scotland.* **Knoxville: University of Tennessee Press, 1977.**

A big volume of charming, funny, and poignant folk songs, including verses and melodies (no piano part or guitar chords).

Pegg, Bob. *Folk: A Portrait of English Traditional Music, Musicians, and Customs.* **London: Wildwood House, 1976.**

Besides discussing the origins of English music traditions and the settings in which different kinds of music are used, the book also includes the notation for some dance tunes and ballads.

Sharp, Cecil. *The Crystal Spring: English Folk Songs.* **Oxford: Oxford University Press, 1987.**

Famous folksong scholar Cecil Sharp presents over 100

of England's most popular traditional songs, printed as melodies with guitar chords.

Van der Horst, Brian. *Folk Music in America.* **New York: F. Watts, 1972.**

What came to be known in the 1960s as the "Folk Scene" really had its roots in traditional British music that traveled to America with immigrants.

Williams, W. S. Gwynn. *Welsh National Music and Dance.* **London: J. Curwen, 1971.**

This two-volume set considers the music forms from medieval Wales that are still the foundation of today's Welsh national music. It includes descriptions of musical structures, harp-playing methods, and as the *penillion*, a unique Welsh style in which a singer improvises a counterpoint to a harp melody.

Williamson, Robin. *The Penny-Whistle Book.* **New York: Oak, 1977.**

"Penny" whistles now cost about eight dollars, and they're available at almost any music store in the United States They are one of the oldest instruments from Britain, and very easy to learn. Williamson gives basic instructions for beginners, written-out melodies of pretty English folk songs, and suggestions for advanced players.

RECORDINGS

Abbot, O. J. *Irish and British Songs from the Ottawa Valley.* **New York: Folkways, 1961.**

Britain's roots in Canada are as old as those in America. Sometimes with guitar and sometimes unaccompanied, Abbot sings ballads that traversed the ocean and took on lives of their own in the New World.

Cuff, Tony. *When First I Went to Caledonia.* **Glasgow: Iona, 1988.**

This singing Scotsman presents a quiet, charming album of songs from his native land, as well as some Scots-

American pieces. Includes a couple of instrumental tracks on guitar and tin whistle.

Discover Scotland. Glasgow: Scotdisc, 1988.

This record is a compilation of many styles of Scottish traditional music. It includes several tunes by Highland bagpipe bands as well as some instrumental and vocal music from the Lowlands.

Ensemble for Early Music. Christmas in Anglia. New York: Nonsuch, 1979.

Frederick Renz directs a small ensemble of voices and Renaissance instruments in this delightful recording of early English holiday music. The tracks span the thirteenth through the eighteenth centuries, including some familiar carols that are surprisingly old.

Folk Music from Nova Scotia. New York: Folkways, 1956.

Nova Scotia is Latin for "New Scotland," and that is very much what this eastern piece of Canada became when it was settled in the seventeenth century. The historians at Folkways Records roamed both rural and city areas looking for keepers of the Scottish Canadian oral tradition.

Folk Music in America. Washington, DC: Library of Congress, 1978.

A multi-CD set culled from the Library of Congress' impressive Archive of Folk Song. Much of this music is clearly influenced by British folk traditions.

Gaughan, Dick. Handful of Earth. El Cerrito, CA: Advent, 1981.

Listen to Dick Gaughan to get a feel for urban life in early industrial Scotland. Inspired by his radical '60s sensibilities, Gaughan sings rough laborers' songs about poor working conditions, rich union officials, and racism in hiring.

George, Siwsann. *Traditional Songs of Wales.* **Wotton-Under-Edge, U.K.: Saydisc, 1994.**

A charming CD featuring love songs, work songs, and popular ballads both in Welsh and English.

The Golden Voices of Wales. **New York: London Records, 1977.**

Welsh music is often associated with religious worship. It's true that much of the most beautiful vocal music to come from Wales are the rich-sounding chorales sung by Nonconformist denominations there.

Jones, Nick. *Ballads and Songs.* **Redditch, Worcestershire, U.K.: Trailer, 1970.**

With a strange, nasal voice and amazing guitar chops, Nick Jones sings British ballads the old-fashioned, mesmerizing way. This is one of his first albums and the most straightforward in production (just voice and acoustic guitar). After a few more records, his career was cut short by a crippling accident.

Larner, Sam. *Now Is the Time for Fishing.* **New York: Folkways, 1961.**

Having lived all his life in Winterton, East Anglia, Sam Larner learned well the beautiful and haunting oral traditions of that fishing village. Here he holds forth in story and song.

Lumbering Songs from the Ontario Shanties. **New York: Folkways, 1961.**

The lumber camps of Ontario, Canada, were full of immigrant workers from England and Scotland. It is clear in these songs how much the traditions that developed in Anglo-Canadian music owed to the old homeland.

Mountain Music Played on the Autoharp. **New York: Folkways, 1962.**

The Appalachian Mountains were populated largely by working-class British immigrants. Because of their isolation, these people developed a unique music tradition based on British dance tunes, with some German fiddling influence. Here some of these lovely melodies are played on an instrument invented in America.

Norman, Chris. *Man with the Wooden Flute.* Troy, NY: Dorian, 1992.

A CD of traditional music of the British Isles, the United States, Quebec, and Cape Breton. Norman plays a traditional instrument made of boxwood, which sounds somewhat like a recorder.

Ossian. *Dove Across the Water.* Glasgow: Iona, 1982.

Ossian is a Scottish band with Irish influence, featuring harp, Irish drum, Irish pipes, guitar, and other instruments to accompany traditional songs. Most of their albums also have long instrumental tracks showing clearly the influence Celtic music has had on developing New Age Jazz.

***Pipes and Drums of Innes Tartan.* Southwater, U.K.: Olympia, 1990.**

No Scottish record collection is complete without a military tattoo. Here's one of the finest, piping and drumming such Scottish march favorites as "Scotland the Brave" and "Athol Highlanders," and everyone's favorite bagpipe hymn, "Amazing Grace."

Redpath, Jean. *Song of the Seals.* London: Philo Records, 1978.

There is no greater Scottish balladeer than Jean Redpath. As much scholar as singer, she sings the songs she finds with as much historical accuracy as possible and always includes notes about the traditions that produced them.

Silly Wizard. *So Many Partings.* Ho-Ho-Kus, NJ: Shanachie, 1980.

While somewhat dated now, Silly Wizard is still fun to listen to. It was among the first bands to plug in Celtic music. This early album features their acoustic chops and beautiful Scottish songs more than their electronic tricks.

Steeleye Span. *Portfolio.* **Newton, NJ: Shanachie, 1988.**

The piercing, powerful voice of Maddy Prior and good instrumentals are what drive this English band's popularity. Add to that some really good songs, often quite creepy, culled from tradition, and you've got one of the most successful British folk groups ever.

Stewart, Andy M. *By the Hush.* **Redditch, Worcestershire, U.K.: Highland, 1982.**

Stewart is a Scotsman with English and Irish roots. In his first solo album he combines traditional music and his own songs to celebrate his heritage with his lovely voice.

Tannahill Weavers. *Tannahill Weavers IV.* **New Canaan, CT: Green Linnett Records, 1982.**

The "Tannies," as they're known, still pack a punch with their great playing, raucous songs, and electric bass. However, they have never recaptured the raging power they possessed in the early '80s when one of their members was the bagpiper Alan MacLeod. The result of those Tannies/MacLeod albums was some wild traditional Scottish rock 'n' roll.

Trimble, Gerald. *First Flight.* **New Canaan, CT: Green Linnet Records, 1983.**

Trimble is an American with Irish and Scottish roots. He plays a family of instruments related to the mandolin, and on this solo album his skillful renditions of many traditional British dance tunes makes one wonder whether he has only ten fingers.

Two-Way Trip: American, Scots, and English Folksongs. **New York: Folkways, 1961.**

It is not surprising that the music of early America was

similar to the traditional music of England and Scotland. What is not so obvious is that the new British American traditions then influenced the musical folk styles in the United Kingdom.

Chapter 5
Getting Started

Learning about the history of your ancestors' home countries is a valuable part of genealogy. Having a vivid image of the times and conditions surrounding the emigration keeps your research from becoming a dull drill in looking up names and numbers. There's a problem, though: First you have to find out where your ancestors came from and how their descendants—your living relatives—got to be who and where they are today.

Family history research is often compared to working as a private investigator. Whether you fancy Agatha Christie's Miss Marple or find tough Mickey Spillane more your speed, keeping the image of your favorite gumshoe in mind while you work can sustain a sense of humor when the going gets tough. Genealogy really is a kind of detective work. Sherlock Holmes is faced with a murder and has to re-create the crime scene by gathering clues and fitting them together. You are trying to write a family history, and your "clues" are the names, dates, places, relationships, and events you find during your research. But just finding the clues is only half the fun. Like the great detective of Baker Street, you need to make sense out of those many facts until they tell a story.

Unlike a private detective, you have nothing at stake and no deadline for completing your investigation. As a beginner at genealogy, it is best to get out of your mind the concept of "completing" your family history. Filling in an entire family tree and writing a family history is a job that can take decades, as well as a lot of money. Some people decide to make this investment because it's really a labor of love. You, too, may find that genealogy is so fascinating that you can't stop. But first, you need to get a start.

Your first task will be to trace your family history back to the ancestor who first arrived in America. These descendants of the Pilgrims celebrate their heritage by dressing as their ancestors did and participating in a memorial service.

There are some rules of thumb that can make family history research more fun and less frustrating:

- Start with what you know. You know your own name, birth date, where you've lived, and other basic information. It may seem silly, but write down every statistic you can think of about yourself. Ask each of your siblings and your parents for the same information about themselves. If you gather all the available facts about the people in your household, it will serve as a springboard to expand your search to other relatives and to previous generations.
- Give yourself a break if you're stuck. Instead of being obsessed with getting every crumb of information about every ancestor, choose one family line and see how far back you can go. Find out everything you can about that line without driving yourself crazy. If your research becomes so boring or frustrating that it isn't fun anymore, give it a rest. Take up another family line for a while.
- Move back in time step by step. Unfortunately, family history research is not quite like an episode of *Doctor Who* or a sequel to *Back to the Future*. If you try to jump back a couple of centuries and start your search in seventeenth century England, you'll find yourself lost in space. Start your search here and now, and follow the clues back through the generations.
- A little genealogy is worth a lot. You don't have to complete a multibranched family tree going back to 1530 in order to learn a lot about your past. Just getting to know where your ancestors came from and in what period they arrived in America can give you a whole new sense of your roots.

Getting Organized

American genealogy is different from that in many other countries. Almost everyone here has roots traceable to somewhere else. Only the Native Americans have a really long history on this continent. Therefore, an American doing family history must proceed in two segments: First he or she must trace the family line back to the "original immigrant ancestor" who came to the United States to begin with, and then take the search further back in that immigrant's native land.

If your original immigrant ancestor was from Britain, the second half of your search will be much easier than if your roots were elsewhere. This is not to say that any family history work is easy, but consider your advantages: English will be the primary language you deal with. Most documents will be in English (you'll run into some Latin, Gaelic, and Welsh), and the librarians and other officials whose help you may depend on will speak your native tongue. Also, Britain has extensive records going back many centuries. True, there are gaps in these records, and their content has been controlled only since the mid-nineteenth century, but any record at all is a gift to a genealogist. You can also expect cooperation once you have extended your search back to your immigrant ancestor's home country. The English, Scots, and Welsh are known for their love of family history.

But first, there is plenty of business to be taken care of on this side of the Atlantic. Let's consider some of the basic concepts behind a genealogical search. You will find that, if you do continue your search in Britain, these general guidelines are still applicable.

The basic premise of genealogy is that you want to find out, by working backward, every person who has contributed to your family tree. Start by thinking about your own family group. Whether or not you live with them or even know them, you have two biological parents. Let's say, for clarity's sake, that they're married and they raised you together. Each of your parents also has two parents, and each of your four grandparents also has two parents, and so on back through the centuries. Now, let's make it more complicated: Each of your two parents has some brothers and sisters. Several of those brothers and sisters are married and have children. Every time one of your aunts and uncles gets married, she or he adds a new surname to the family tree. Your uncle may give his wife his surname when he marries, but that does not erase the many surnames that come together to make up *her* family tree. They all become a part of your family history by marriage to one of your kin.

At every level of a family tree there are branches that account for the siblings, marriages, children, and remarriages at each generation. When traced thoroughly, this can involve hundreds of surnames, with hundreds of people in each surname. How on earth can you possibly keep track of all these people?

Fortunately for you, genealogy has been around a long time. Family researchers have developed clever, efficient ways for finding, organizing, and using information in a lineage search. Although you can buy all sorts of fancy research supplies custom-made for genealogists, that kind of expense is completely unnecessary for a person dabbling in research for the first time. The tools you absolutely must have are the sorts of thing you need for school anyway: loose-leaf paper and a big three-ring binder with alphabetized dividers. If you can afford it, manila folders with tabs you can label are also very useful.

Genealogy involves taking lots of notes and making copies of documents that are of use to you. It's not a bad idea to empty out a drawer or find a big box that you can devote to nothing but your family research files. The more organized you are at every step, the more fun the project will be. Nothing puts a damper on your attitude like being sure you've got so-and-so's birth certificate but not being able to find it when you need it. Starting off with a simple, clear filing system will help you avoid that kind of trouble.

Family Group Sheets and Pedigree Charts

One excellent innovation that was the result of family historians' trial and error was the advent of standardized forms. You can get these forms, meant to help you organize essential information about each individual and family, in several ways. The most expensive "professional-looking" way is to order the forms from a genealogical supplier. Addresses for ordering forms are given at the end of this chapter. You can also go to a research library with a genealogy department and pay twenty-five cents or fifty cents for a copy of each form, which you can then photocopy as you need them. The least expensive option is to get a book from the library that shows a facsimile of the forms you need, and then draw similar forms yourself.

Two basic forms are used in family research: family group sheets and pedigree charts. You can supplement them by many other pages of notes and organized information sheets, but these are the essentials. Examples of these charts are shown on the following pages.

A family group sheet shows a single marriage/couple and the children from that marriage. Try making one for yourself. You will need the following information: The name, date of birth, and place of birth for you, all your siblings, and both of your biological parents. (It doesn't matter if that nuclear family doesn't live as a unit. Genealogy traces genetic lines only. You can always fill in details about who lived with whom once you write up a family history.) You will also need the marriage date of your parents. If one of your birth parents is deceased, you will need his or her date of death and place of burial. If one of your parents is remarried, you should make a separate group sheet for that marriage and the kids from it.

A pedigree chart consolidates the information you get from all the family group sheets you make. It is a timeline stretching from you back to the earliest generation you can get facts on. Each time you get information from a family group sheet, fill it in on your pedigree chart. Take the chart with you every time you do research, so you always know what names or dates you're still missing.

Sounds pretty straightforward, right? Here's the problem that turns genealogy into a big research project: You have to have proof of everything. Your dad can tell you he was born at St. Joseph's Hospital in Phoenix on July 22, 1946, and of course you believe him. But it is not considered a fact in genealogy until you have seen his birth certificate. Every

A British American Photo Album

Dissatisfaction with the monarchy, religious persecution, and the quest for better economic conditions were among the factors that prompted English, Scottish, and Welsh emigrants to leave their homeland for a "new world." Some left behind the teeming industrial cities of England; others, the impoverished countryside of Scotland and Wales. Today, the majority of Americans have at least one family line that can be traced to Britain. The American cities of New York, New London, Birmingham, Rochester, Durham, Greenwich, and many others are testament to the firm roots of British influence on American soil. Much has changed since the first British immigrants landed on American shores. Britain itself, of course, has changed. Yet Americans and Britons alike continue to celebrate their British heritage, the beauty and variety of the United Kingdom, and the richness of its history, culture, and institutions.

North Atlantic Ocean

SCOTLAND

Aberdeen

Glasgow   Edinburgh

North Channel

Durham

ENGLAND

ISLE OF MAN

Irish Sea

Preston

Manchester

Liverpool

Dublin

Matlock   Lincoln

IRELAND

Gwynedd

Stafford   Nottingham

Norwich

Leicester

Birmingham

Cambridge

Ipswich

WALES   Gloucester

Cardiff   Oxford   Hertford

London

Bristol

Kingston

Taunton   Winchester

Exeter   Dorchester

Truro   English Channel

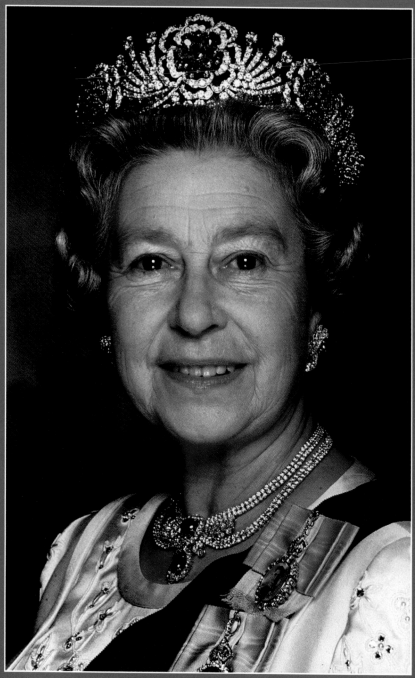

The role of the British royal family in the second half of the twentieth century has been largely symbolic, prompting some people to speculate on whether the monarchy is an anachronistic institution that no longer serves a purpose. Outdated though it may be, the notion of royalty still holds appeal for Britons and others around the world. Queen Elizabeth II, the reigning monarch, poses for a recent official portrait.

Settlers in the American colonies resented the monarchical system of inherited rule and what they perceived as the King's oppressive interference in their political, economic, and religious affairs. This 1857 painting by William Walcutt captures the rage of the colonists as they tore down the statue of George III in New York City during the Revolutionary War.

England is home to some of the world's most renowned academic institutions. Cambridge University was founded at the beginning of the thirteenth century. Students live and study at more than twenty residential colleges that make up the university.

The British Parliament meets in this building on the Thames River. The British notion of representative government, which has roots in the royal councils that advised medieval kings, has served as a model for governments all over the world, including that of the United States.

The Tower of London is an ancient complex of buildings on the north bank of the Thames River.
When it served as a prison, it housed luminaries such as Lady Jane Grey, Sir Thomas More,
Anne Boleyn, and Sir Walter Raleigh. Today, the Crown Jewels are displayed at the Tower
in an underground vault. The vault contains crowns, scepters, many pieces of jewelry, and
precious gems collected by the royal family over the centuries.

The distinctive uniform of the palace guard is a sight commonly associated with England—like London's red double-decker buses. The traditional changing-of-the-guard ceremony at Buckingham Palace, pictured here, still takes place regularly. The guards are soldiers in the British army who serve at the palace as part of their military service.

Today's London is a bustling, modern city. While it has its share of problems, like all large cities, they do not approach the horrific conditions that characterized some of the city's neighborhoods during the Industrial Revolution. Many workers who toiled under these conditions in London and other British cities abandoned their jobs for ships to the United States.

Immigrant groups have long diversified the British population, contributing to the increasingly multicultural face of London.

Great Britain is much more than London, of course. As you will no doubt discover in your own genealogical research, Wales, Scotland, and England are intertwined historically and culturally yet still maintain distinct identities. The scenery in Gwynedd, in northern Wales, is typical of an area where dairy farming and sheep-raising are the major economic activities. South Wales, by contrast, is heavily industrialized.

A spectator turned out in traditional Welsh costume at the investiture of Prince Charles as Prince of Wales in 1969.

Tartans and bagpipes are among the most recognizable Scottish symbols. The Scots themselves are proud and celebratory of their heritage, with events such as the Glasgow Highland Games, where a Scottish girl displays her highland dancing skills.

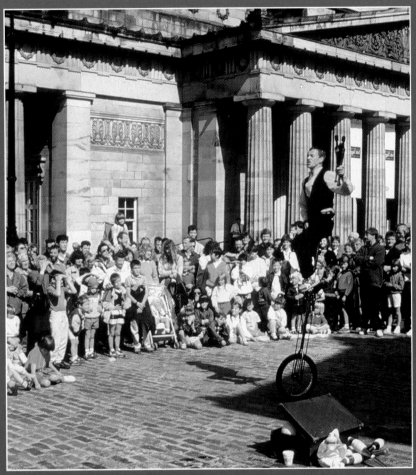

A street performer entertains crowds at Scotland's Edinburgh Festival. Over 640,000 people live in the Edinburgh metropolitan area.

The Notting Hill Carnival is a celebration of cultural diversity, with music, dance, and foods from around the world. Great Britain, like the United States, comprises citizens of varying ethnic origin, particularly from former British colonies.

Carnival participants of all ethnicities, swept away by the festivities, dance in the streets.

Perhaps one of your goals in your genealogical search is eventually to travel to Britain—where you might have the opportunity to meet distant relatives you've traced. You may even find you feel an instant affinity for the land and people to whom you have an important connection.

Pedigree Chart

Name of Compiler _____

Address _____

City, State _____

Date _____

Person No.1 on this chart is the same person as No._____ on chart No._____.

Chart No._____

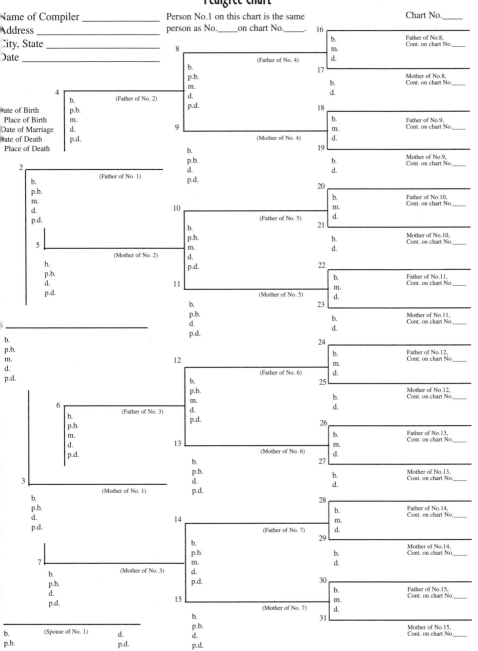

8 (Father of No. 4)
b.
p.b.
m.
d.
p.d.

4 (Father of No. 2)
b.
p.b.
m.
d.
p.d.

9 (Mother of No. 4)
b.
p.b.
d.
p.d.

Date of Birth
Place of Birth
Date of Marriage
Date of Death
Place of Death

2 (Father of No. 1)
b.
p.b.
m.
d.
p.d.

5 (Mother of No. 2)
b.
p.b.
d.
p.d.

10 (Father of No. 5)
b.
p.b.
m.
d.
p.d.

11 (Mother of No. 5)
b.
p.b.
d.
p.d.

b.
p.b.
m.
d.
p.d.

6 (Father of No. 3)
b.
p.b.
m.
d.
p.d.

12 (Father of No. 6)
b.
p.b.
m.
d.
p.d.

13 (Mother of No. 6)
b.
p.b.
d.
p.d.

3 (Mother of No. 1)
b.
p.b.
d.
p.d.

7 (Mother of No. 3)
b.
p.b.
d.
p.d.

14 (Father of No. 7)
b.
p.b.
m.
d.
p.d.

15 (Mother of No. 7)
b.
p.b.
d.
p.d.

(Spouse of No. 1)
b.
p.b.
d.
p.d.

16
b.
m.
d.
Father of No.8,
Cont. on chart No._____

17
b.
d.
Mother of No.8,
Cont. on chart No._____

18
b.
m.
d.
Father of No.9,
Cont. on chart No._____

19
b.
d.
Mother of No.9,
Cont. on chart No._____

20
b.
m.
d.
Father of No.10,
Cont. on chart No._____

21
b.
d.
Mother of No.10,
Cont. on chart No._____

22
b.
m.
d.
Father of No.11,
Cont. on chart No._____

23
b.
d.
Mother of No.11,
Cont. on chart No._____

24
b.
m.
d.
Father of No.12,
Cont. on chart No._____

25
b.
d.
Mother of No.12,
Cont. on chart No._____

26
b.
m.
d.
Father of No.13,
Cont. on chart No._____

27
b.
d.
Mother of No.13,
Cont. on chart No._____

28
b.
m.
d.
Father of No.14,
Cont. on chart No._____

29
b.
d.
Mother of No.14,
Cont. on chart No._____

30
b.
m.
d.
Father of No.15,
Cont. on chart No._____

31
b.
d.
Mother of No.15,
Cont. on chart No._____

FAMILY GROUP WORK SHEET #_____

HUSBAND, Name:		WIFE, Name:	
Birth:	Place:	Birth:	Place:
Death:	Place:	Death:	Place:
Burial:	Place:	Burial:	Place:
Father:		Father:	
Mother:		Mother:	
Occupation:		Occupation:	
Notes:		Notes:	

Name	Date & Place of Birth	Marriage	Date & Place of Death	Married to	Date & Place of Birth Death

time you get a piece of information to write on a family group sheet, you must also write down exactly where you got that information. That way, if there are discrepancies later, you will be able to double-check sources or make decisions about which source is more reliable. This won't be a problem with your own household, but it may be a big issue when you're trying to find out in what year your great-grandfather was born.

Birth, death, and marriage certificates fall into a category of documents called vital records. In the United States these are available from the courthouse in the county where the event took place. There may be a small fee for retrieving a document. You can write to the Government Printing Office at the address at the end of this chapter for more information on obtaining vital records. For information on baptisms, christenings, bar mitzvahs, and other religious events, you should contact the church or synagogue where the event took place, if possible. Such records may also be kept at a central archdiocese or parish office.

Each time you get an important document about a person, whether legal or personal, keep that document in a carefully labeled folder containing that person's family group sheet and all other documents relating to that nuclear family. Some people give each family group an identification number, which makes for easier note-taking and organization.

Talking to Relatives

It's not of much use knowing how to get vital records if you don't know where a person was born. Which county courthouse should you write to? Talking to relatives can lead you to this kind of information. Even though what people tell you is not fact until you verify it, relatives' memories may provide the only path to certain documents.

At least as important as the facts they can remember are the emotions, the stories, the legends that fill your relatives' memories. They can flesh out the names and dates from a marriage certificate. They might remember attending the christening or funeral that you only have preserved on a legal form. They can tell you things that no written document has ever preserved: the personal character of your kin. Where else will you find out about an ancestor's twinkling eyes, favorite flavor of ice cream, favorite big-band tune, or teasing sense of humor?

Interviewing relatives can lead to such a wealth of information and inspiration that it's a good way to begin a genealogical search. Poll your family to develop a list of all the relatives they know about and try to talk or write to every one. As your search goes on, you will find out about more people who are kin to you, and you can add them to your interview list.

Family historians agree that the best way to approach your relatives for information is to write a letter to each one you know about, asking if he or she would be willing to help you with your family history. Assure the person that you will share your family history with him or her, and underscore how much you would appreciate cooperation with your search. It's a good idea to include a list of questions you have already formulated, so the relative can give them some thought before you talk to him or her. That also gives your relative the option of writing in reply if a personal or telephone interview is not possible. Include a copy of the pedigree chart that you're working on, to see how they react to what you've already found. Differences of opinion about family facts can lead to some very interesting discoveries.

The questions you send can be standardized for the many relatives you contact. Type out the questions, then photocopy them. Remember to leave plenty of room for answers. Some of your questions should be very specific. For example:

> I am tracing the MacAlistair line of our family. The earliest family member I have found is Gordon MacAlistair, who lived in Baltimore from 1909 to 1940. Do you have any information on his birthplace or date, or his parents or any earlier relatives?

You should also include some general questions. Assure the respondent that even vague information is helpful. You might ask the following:

- Are you aware of the existence of any personal papers, letters, bibles, or diaries belonging to any member of the family? Do you have any idea where they might be kept?
- Do you know whether anyone in the family has already done any genealogy research? This could in-

clude pedigree charts, family trees, personal memoirs, or biographical descriptions of anyone in the family.

- Do you know if anyone in the family's past was in the military service, either in the United States or Britain? Please list what branch of the military he/she served in, and the approximate years of service.
- Can you think of any farmland, estate land, houses, or any other real estate owned by the family in the past?
- Who are the earliest family members you have heard of? Where and when did they live?
- Was anyone in the family notable in his or her career, and might he or she be listed in books like *Who's Who*? Did any relatives get advanced university degrees?
- Can you recall any photographs, daguerreotypes, or portraits of any family members? Who might have those now?

If you can afford it, enclose a self-addressed stamped postcard or envelope with each letter you write. People are more likely to respond when they don't have to worry about writing out an address or finding a stamp. Telephone interviews can be very expensive, so it's better to use the mail for long-distance interviews. The best approach is to make up a questionnaire based on queries you have about your own research. Concentrate on the areas where you need information and where this particular relative is likely to have an answer (or at least an opinion). Ask about people he probably knew and events he may have attended. Don't forget to ask for other names, dates, or places that can lead to more clues. Does your relative have any neighbors who knew the ancestor you're inquiring about? Perhaps you could arrange to contact them. What schools did the ancestor attend? What company did he work for? They might still have useful records.

The best interview is one that takes place in person. If you are lucky enough to have relatives living nearby or can travel to see them, you are at an advantage. If they agree to be interviewed, you can talk to them in their own homes while they sit in their favorite chairs and reminisce. Come prepared with focused questions, but don't stop them from rambling from subject to subject. In this way you can pick up connections you never dreamed of and also get some good stories to spice up your family history.

If you have or can borrow a tape recorder, always ask your subject if you may record the interview. If possible, take a camcorder and videotape it. When you get home, transcribe your conversation from the tape so you can refer to it easily. Some answering machines allow a telephone interview to be recorded, but remember that it is illegal to record a phone conversation without the other party's permission. It is a nice gesture to write a summary of the interview once you have studied your transcription and send it to the subject, along with a letter of thanks. He or she may write back with corrections, which can be valuable to you.

Treasures from the Attic

Interviewing a relative can lead to more than just facts and stories. Always be sure to ask whether there are any old papers or heirlooms that you may see. Some people are real pack rats, and nothing helps a family historian like a pack rat. You may find anything from a set of pewter spoons brought over from England to the only surviving photograph of your great-grandfather's wedding.

Most older people are flattered that a young person is interested in their past, so you may find yourself allowed access to some keepsakes that have been gathering dust for decades. Keep your eye out for any official-looking documents. Marriage, birth, death, or military certificates, tax forms, school diplomas, report cards, evaluations from work, wills, even old bills—all these have a tendency to be put in boxes and stuffed into attics or back closets. They can be valuable sources of information.

Official documents are essential to genealogy, but many of them can be found in more than one place if you search hard enough. The real treasures of your relatives' storage

You may find that you can spot family resemblances by looking at old photos. It is also interesting to look at the way people dressed and how they expressed themselves in photographs.

boxes are the unique personal items that can never be replaced. Diaries, letters, family bibles, photographs, handicrafts, scrapbooks, and baby books yield more than just information. They can turn a cold research project into a personal quest for real people. It's exciting to find an ancestor's birth certificate, but opening a trunk and finding the bagpipes your great-great-grandfather insisted on bringing with him to the United States in 1882 is like being able to reach out and touch the past.

Resources

ORGANIZING

American Genealogy: A Basic Course. **National Genealogical Society.**

> Write to NGS at 4527 17th Street North, Arlington, VA 22207-2363 for a brochure about this home-study program. It includes written and video material and is a great way to learn about organization and research skills before you hit the libraries.

Banaka, William H. *Training in Depth Interviewing.* **New York: Harper & Row, 1971.**

> Skilled interviewing isn't just a matter of sitting down and chatting. This book contains tips for preparing, staying focused, and getting good answers from the interviewee.

Board for Certification of Genealogists
P.O. Box 5816 Falmouth, VA 22403-5816.

> Send a self-addressed stamped envelope and three dollars for a current list of certified family history researchers.

Directory of Professional Genealogists. **Salt Lake City: Association of Professional Genealogists, 1994.**

> Although most people cannot afford to hire a professional researcher, it is good to know where to find one if your search ever gets to such an advanced level that you need help with sticky problems.

Dollarhide, William. *Managing a Genealogical Project: A Complete Manual for the Management and Organization of Genealogical Materials.* **Baltimore: Genealogical Publishing, 1988.**

Common sense and lots of labeled folders are sometimes not enough to keep a novice family researcher organized. Take advantage of Dollarhide's vast experience; he's also responsible for designing the best computer software for the organization of genealogical projects.

A Handy Book for Genealogists. Logan, UT: Everton Publishers, 1989.

Everton is one of the biggest publishers of genealogical books and magazines for Americans. This is a good start-up guide from the pros.

Heritage Quest. American Genealogical Lending Library.

The AGLL publishes this bimonthly magazine. In addition to the usual classified ads offering or seeking information and services, *Heritage Quest* features columns on computer technology and adoption searches.

Schreiner-Yantis, Netti. *Genealogical and Local History Books in Print.*, 3 vols., 4th ed. Springfield, VA: Schreiner-Yantis, 1990.

This not only catalogs some hard-to-find manuscripts related to family research; it also lists vendors in the United States who sell various publications, supplies, and services of use to the genealogist.

Schreiner-Yantis Family Group Sheets

Netti Schreiner-Yantis designed what is considered the best family group sheet available, as well as pedigree charts and other forms. Write for a price list. GBIP, 6818 Lois Drive, Springfield, VA 22150.

Stano, Michael E., and Reinsch, N. L., Jr. *Communication in Interviews.* Englewood Cliffs, NJ: Prentice-Hall, 1982.

These communication arts experts offer advice on interviewing that can be applied to family history chats with your relatives. They discuss ways to prepare before your talk, how to communicate your questions clearly, and how to read important signals (for example, if your relative is trying to tell you that a certain subject is uncomfortable to talk about).

Wasserman, P., and Kennington, A., eds. *Ethnic Information Sources of the United States.* **Detroit: Gale Research, 1976.**

An amazing sourcebook listing fraternities, cultural and educational organizations, heritage institutes, and information on libraries and archives around the country and the strengths of their specific collections.

AMERICAN GENEALOGICAL SOCIETIES

American Genealogical Lending Library
593 West North Street
P.O. Box 329
Bountiful, UT 84011

AGLL offers an extremely useful service: It rents microforms of indexes (vital records, censuses, etc.) for a reasonable fee. Even if you can't afford to become a member—and it's highly improbable that you have a microfilm projector in your house—you might be able to persuade your local library to participate in AGLL rental programs. Little by little, these indexes are also coming out on CD-ROM, and are for sale.

Association for State and Local History
172 Second Avenue North
Nashville, TN 37201

Write for a list of publications, and check a research library for a copy of its Directory of Historical Organizations in the United States and Canada. This is not specifically for genealogists, but the two subjects overlap considerably.

The Augustan Society, Inc.
1510 Cravens Avenue
Torrance, CA 90501

This is a society of Scottish Americans and English Americans who publish the *Scottish-American Genealogist* and *English Genealogist*, and offer other publications and research assistance. They also act as a registry for Scottish clan members in the United States.

Central Texas Genealogical Society Bulletin

This quarterly stopped publication in 1971, but it's worth checking its index for information on ancestors who migrated to Texas. Many British people went to that state to seek work in the mid-nineteenth century.

Meyer, Mary K. *Meyer's Directory of Genealogical Societies in the USA and Canada.* Mt. Airy, MD: Mary K. Meyer, 1988.

Check this book in a genealogical library to find out which societies have activities in your region, focus on your family's ethnic group and settlement area, publish useful catalogs and manuals, and have reasonable membership fees.

National Genealogical Society
4527 17th Street North
Arlington, VA 22207-2363

One of the biggest American family research associations, the NGS publishes and sells books, forms, and indexes. Membership entitles you to the *National Genealogical Society Quarterly* and *NGS Newsletter*.

National Institute on Genealogical Research
P.O. Box 14274
Washington, DC 20044-4274

Although membership in this organization is more useful to experienced genealogists, it is worth writing to them for information on their publications and workshops. Also, keep the name in mind; if you see its imprint on a book or index you know you can trust that source.

PATRIOTIC SOCIETIES

These organizations exist to serve American descendants of soldiers and statemen and act as custodians of records. If you can trace an ancestor to the period of the struggle for independence from Britain, it may be worthwhile to contact one of these groups:

Descendants of the Signers of the Declaration of Independence
1300 Locust Street
Philadelphia, PA 19107

National Society
Daughters of the American Revolution
1776 D Street NW
Washington, DC 20006

National Society
Sons of the American Revolution
2412 Massachusetts Avenue
Washington, DC 20008

STARTING YOUR SEARCH

United States
Evelyn Spears Family Group Sheet Exchange
East 12502 Frideger Street
Elk, WA 99009

> A service that provides previously researched family group sheets for the requested surname. About ten dollars per surname, with a catalog of 14,000 surnames.

Genealogical Center, Inc.
International Family Group Sheet Exchange
P.O. Box 17698
Tampa, FL 33682

> This service charges thirty cents per page, and each completed surname study is anywhere from 10 to 300 pages long. Write for catalog of 8,000 surnames.

Genealogical Quarterly. **London: Research Publishing Co.**

> Formerly called *Topographical Quarterly*, this periodical deals with family and local history issues in both Britain and America. Many of the people who write for it are members of the Federation of Family History Societies

and offer an experienced view of family research in England.

Greenwood, Val D. *The Researcher's Guide to American Genealogy.* **Baltimore: Genealogical Publishing, 1990.**

Professional genealogists recommend this book as a starting point that can lead you into an intermediate level of research and then guide you toward more advanced resources.

Hilton, Suzanne. *Who Do You Think You Are? Digging for Your Family Roots.* **Philadelphia: Westminster Press, 1977.**

Although you'll want to go to more recent sources eventually, this one remains a good place to start a general search because it's written for young people. It includes practical introductions to using British libraries and archives in person.

Kirkham, E. Kay. *The Handwriting of American Records for a Period of 300 Years.* **Logan, UT: Everton Publishers, 1973.**

Before the advent of typewriters, legal documents were written by hand. Even when they were prepared by someone with really good handwriting (which was often not the case), there were many differences in penmanship practices between the eighteenth century and now, making key words difficult to decipher.

Scotland

Bede, Tim. *MacRoots: How to Trace Your Scottish Ancestors.* **Edinburgh: Macdonald, 1982.**

A light-hearted introduction for the genealogical novice. It includes a good overview of the clan system and how to trace true clan members and septs.

Coppage, A. Maxim. *Searching for Scottish Ancestors.* **Utica, KY: McDowell Publications, 1983.**

A manual for finding out whether you have Scottish roots and following them to the source. Includes maps showing surname settlement patterns both in Scotland and America.

Hamilton-Edwards, Gerald. *In Search of Scottish Ancestry.* **London: Philimore, 1972.**

A thorough introduction to the practice of Scottish family research as well as some background in Scottish history and immigration. Principally devoted to the official records available from the New Register House in Edinburgh, but it also deals at some length with the House of Lyons and the Scottish heraldry system.

James, Alwyn. *Scottish Roots: A Step-by-Step Guide for Ancestor Hunters.* **Gretna, LA: Pelican Publications, 1982.**

First published in Scotland, this handbook has been expanded to start the search in America. It explains how to discover whether any of your ancestors were Scottish, and how to proceed depending on the class (convict, worker, merchant, nobleman) and area from which your ancestor came.

Scotland: A Genealogical Research Guide. **Salt Lake City: Genealogical Library of The Church of Jesus Christ of Latter-day Saints, 1987.**

The Family History Library of the Mormon Church is the best place in America to turn for records on the British Isles. Here they explain their collection of Scottish documents and how to use them.

Whyte, Donald. *Introducing Scottish Genealogical Research.* **Edinburgh: Scottish Genealogy Society, 1979.**

Step-by-step instructions, including how to use various document types and advice for troubleshooting. This book is especially strong in its description of the Register Houses in Edinburgh where vital statistics, parish, and legal documents are stored.

England/Great Britain

Baxter, Angus. *In Search of Your British and Irish Roots: A Complete Guide to Tracing Your English, Welsh, Scottish, and Irish Ancestors.* **Toronto: Macmillan of Canada, 1982.**

One of the bibles of genealogical research, enthusiastically recommended by reference librarians.

Buckley, Kenneth A. *British Ancestry Tracing: A D.I.Y. Guide for Beginners.* **West Midlands, England: K. A. Buckley, 1978.**

If you can find this little thirty-page opus, it is worth a look for its user-friendly approach to working on a British search. (D.I.Y., if you didn't catch it, is "do it yourself.")

Christmas, Brian. *Sources for One-Name Studies and for Other Family Historians.* **London: Guild of One-Name Studies, 1991.**

One-name historians are those who choose one of their family lines and follow it back as far into the mists of time as possible, rather than filling in some members of a few generations. This approach is sometimes recommended for beginners and is preferred by many experienced researchers.

The English Genealogist. **Torrance, CA: Augustan Society.**

Annual periodical published by a British American society. It is a trusted source for genealogical information, listing new available references and completed and published family histories. Its main interest is in noble lineage and clans.

Family History Sourcebooks

The following reference sets are very useful to check at the beginning of a search to be sure that no one has already published a family history on one of the surnames on your tree. Each has an alphabetical index where your surname(s) would be listed if any such work exists. Remember that these are lists of *published* family histories. If someone did genealogy on your family and didn't publish it or donate it to a library, you will have to hope that you find it among a relative's possessions.

The British Catalog of Printed Books. Landed Gentry. London: HMSO, updated periodically.

Thompson, T. R., ed. *Catalogue of British Family Histories*. London: Research Publishing, updated periodically.

Family History News and Digest. Tollerton, England: Federation of Family History Societies.

Looking at this publication is an efficient way to get a feel for what's happening in British genealogy. The Federation includes organizations from every county in England and many in Scotland and Wales. There are articles and advertisements touching on every corner of the United Kingdom.

Family Tree Magazine

A bimonthly periodical devoted to family history research in Britain. It is a good source for advertisements, both classified (British people seeking information about their surname) and commercial (services offering completed family group sheets, for example).

Fitzhugh, Terrick. *The Dictionary of Genealogy: A Guide to British Ancestry Research*. London: Black, 1991.

Sources, terms, document types, and procedures are listed alphabetically for easy reference. This book is a good complement to a beginner's manual, in case you get stuck on a particular term or concept along the way.

Leary, William. *My Ancestors Were Methodists; How Can I Find Out More About Them?* London: Society of Genealogists, 1990.

A short manual for beginners searching for Methodist ancestors in Britain. The biggest enclave of Methodists was in Wales, and large numbers of that faith either traveled or moved to America between 1700 and 1850.

Loomes, Brian. *The Concise Guide to Tracing Your Ancestry.* **London: Barrie and Jenkins, 1992.**

A succinct yet comprehensive guide to researching one's family history in Britain.

My Ancestor Was Jewish; How Can I Find Out More About Him? **London: Society of Genealogists, 1982.**

British immigrants to America were not all Christian. This book is a good place to find information if your ancestors were Jews in Great Britain. Jews did not make up a huge number of the British emigrants to America, but, since they faced persecution like all other nonconformists, some did come here.

National Genealogical Directory. **Brighton, England: Burchall and Warren, 1992.**

Updated occasionally, this directory is useful for its all-encompassing nature. Societies and researchers are cited from Great Britain, Canada, Australia, and New Zealand.

New England Historical and Genealogical Register. **Boston: New England Historic Genealogical Society.**

A periodical published by the New England Historic Genealogical Society, which has been collecting family history manuscripts since 1845. They have over two million in their collection now.

Northern Genealogists. **York, England: John Sampson.**

This journal, printed from 1895 to 1903, concentrates on the north of England. Although that territory is historically a place of miners and other workers, this journal is more concerned with the pedigree of gentry in the area of Northumbria.

Pattinson, Penelope M. *Directory of Family History Project Coordinators,* **5th ed. Plymouth, England: Federation of Family History Societies, 1984.**

From this directory you can learn the names and addresses of people involved in past and present genealogy projects in Britain. Although many of the projects will have been completed since publication, you can find out the sorts of things the Federation does and see if any apply to your family.

Pelling, George. *Beginning Your Family History*, 5th ed. **Newbury, England: Countryside Books, 1989.**

The Federation of Family History Societies is responsible for this brief introduction to working in Britain and using British sources. Includes advice on exchanging information with members of the Federation.

Saul, Pauline A., and Markwell, F. C. *The A-Z Guide to Tracing Ancestors in Britain.* **Baltimore: Genealogical Publishing, 1991.**

A clear format and a good index mark this manual. It's not as exhaustive as the title claims, but it's a good introduction to British sources, documents, archives, and procedures. Its American publication makes it easier to find in the States.

Steele, Donald John. *Discovering Your Family History.* **London: British Broadcasting Corporation, 1980.**

This is a basic introduction to doing research in England. It covers both old English families as well as those fairly recently arrived in England from other parts of the British Isles.

Watts, Michael J. *My Ancestor Was in the British Army; How Can I Find Out More About Him?* **London: Society of Genealogists, 1992.**

See references in chapter 5 (Libraries and Archives) for more specific books on Army records, but use this one as a brief introduction to the subject. It covers the general principles of finding information on common troops and officers in all branches of the military.

Wales

Bartrum, Peter C. *Welsh Genealogies, A.D. 300–1400*, **8 vols. Cardiff: University of Wales Press, 1974.**

————. *Welsh Genealogies: A.D. 1400–1500*, **18 vols. Aberystwyth: National Library of Wales, 1983.**

Dictionaries of family histories arranged alphabetically by name; each set includes a multivolume index.

Hall, Joseph. *The Genealogical Handbook for England and Wales.* **Salt Lake City: J. Hall, 1977.**

England sought unification with Wales for centuries before it actually occurred. England had sent settlers to Wales as early as the fourteenth century, and Wales had sent its young to England for education. This book deals with family research issues that cross between the two cultures.

Hamilton-Edwards, Gerald. *In Search of Welsh Ancestry.* **Baltimore: Genealogical Publishing, 1986.**

This prolific writer of genealogy books now turns his attention to particularly Welsh matters of family history. Includes good information on sources and procedures, plus background on Welsh names.

Hawkings, David T. *Criminal Ancestors: A Guide to Historical Criminal Records in England and Wales.* **Phoenix Mill, England: Alan Sutton, 1992.**

Learn how to get the skeletons out of your ancestors' closets. Criminal records not only add important information for your family history; they also add spice. Jails were also a prime source of forced emigrants to America.

Rogers, Colin Darlington. *The Family Tree Detective.* **Manchester, England: Manchester University Press, 1983.**

A manual for analyzing and solving research problems in England and Wales. Covers documents since 1538 and the most efficient ways to find elusive relatives.

Rowlands, John, et al., eds. *Welsh Family History: A Guide to Research.* **Aberystwyth: Association of Family History Societies of Wales, 1993.**

This is an excellent guide to doing research in Wales. It is illustrated with maps as well as facsimiles of documents such as wills and deeds, explaining how to read them.

Welsh-American Genealogical Society Newsletter.
Poultney, VT: Welsh-American Genealogical Society.

> A quarterly devoted to issues of Welsh migration and ancestry. Look here for Welsh family group sheet exchanges and information on Welsh names, including upcoming reunions.

VITAL RECORDS AND NAMES

Black, Dr. George F. *The Surnames of Scotland, Their Origin, Meaning and History.* **New York: New York Public Library, 1968.**

> Put together from holdings in this major genealogical research library, this book can help give you a glimpse of the distant past of your Scottish family lines. Includes maps showing the settlement patterns of clans and noble families.

Camp, Anthony. *Everyone Has Roots.* **Baltimore: Genealogical Publishing: 1978.**

> This introduction to genealogy is especially useful because of its information about surname changes in the British Isles.

General Register House
St. Catherine's House
100 Kingsway
London WC2D 6JB

> For civil records since they started being collected in 1837, this is the most efficient central resource, rather than contacting the specific district where your ancestor lived. Write to them with information on the ancestor's name and any places and dates you've found so far.

Health Resources Administration
National Center for Health Statistics
Rockville, MD 20852

> Write for a form to order certificates or records of ances-

tors who were U.S. citizens but who died or were born in a foreign country.

Hughes, James Pennethorne. *Is Thy Name Wart? The Origin of Some Curious and Other Surnames.* **London: Phueniy Hoyse, 1965.**

Since the Middle Ages nicknames have sometimes been turned into surnames. The problem, of course, is that a nickname based on a character trait or physical feature might not fit everyone down the line for generations. Includes index of odd surnames.

Kemp, Thomas Jay. *International Vital Records Handbook.* **Baltimore: Genealogical Publishing, 1990.**

Was your great-great-grandfather a manager for the British East India company so your great-grandmother was born in Bangladesh? Don't worry, check this source for how to find unusual records relating to Britain, Canada, and the United States.

Morgan, T. J., and Morgan, Prys. *Welsh Surnames.* **Cardiff: University of Wales Press, 1985.**

Learn how Lloyd became Floyd, and how not to be intimidated by a string of double letters, with only y's and w's as vowels. You will find that most common Welsh surnames today are a combination of ancient Celtic naming practices and Scandinavian, Norman, and English influence.

Noble, Wilfred Vernon. *Nicknames: Past and Present.* **London: H. Hamilton, 1976.**

A knowledge of nicknames throughout history can help you interpret letters and diaries belonging to family members. Someone called "Dobbin" in a letter could be your great-great-uncle Robert. Nicknames also occasionally turn into surnames, and this book will help you use that knowledge to benefit your research.

Parish and Vital Records: List of Genealogical Department of Latter-day Saints. **Salt Lake City: The Church of Jesus Christ of Latter-day Saints, 1985.**

Even experienced professional genealogists in the United Kingdom turn to this list before hitting the index drawers at the General Register House. The LDS Library has transcribed a huge number of the vital records from England, and they're available on microfilm, with some on CD-ROM.

The Registrar General
New Register House
Princes Street
Edinburgh EH1 3YT

Write here with a very specific request for parish registers since the 1500s, vital records since 1855, and the Scottish censuses from 1841 to 1901. Include exactly what records you seek and in what area of Britain you believe your ancestor lived. You might offer alternative spellings of the surname, if you've found any.

Scottish Record Office
H.M. Register House
Princes Street
Edinburgh EH1 3YX

Write here with specific requests for vital records, wills, deeds, and other legal documents. Include the full name of the ancestor, the county where the event took place (birth, death, baptism, etc.), and the approximate year.

The Story of Surnames. **Aylesbury, England: Hazel Watson & Viney, 1965.**

Which British names are French, Norman, Gaelic, Scandinavian? When did surnames come into use in different regions? You can look up the most recent British form of your surname in the index and learn where it came from and how it changed.

Where to Write for Vital Records: Births, Deaths, Marriages and Divorces.

Order this booklet from the U.S. Government Printing Office, Superintendent of Documents, Washington, DC 20402. It costs $3.25. Request a brochure of publications relating to family research.

Withycombe, Elizabeth Gidley. *Oxford Dictionary of English Christian Names.* **Oxford: Oxford University Press, 1977.**

Although it is not recommended that you rely too heavily on first names to help you in your search, unusual ones can lead to clues. Also, learning the meaning of names can help to flesh out the generations that used them and their times.

FAMILY PAPERS AND HEIRLOOMS

Brackman, Barbara. *Clues in the Calico: Identifying and Dating Quilts.* **McLean, VA: EPM Publications, 1989.**

A quilt made by the hands of your ancestor can really bring history to life. Certain patterns, sewing styles, color choices, and material types act as identifying marks to the trained eye.

Earnest, Russell D. *Grandma's Attic: Making Heirlooms Part of Your Family History.* **Albuquerque, NM: R. D. Earnest Assoc., 1991.**

Letters and diaries aren't the only important things you'll find in a relative's storage area. This book helps you recognize the significance of other objects once owned by your ancestors, such as china, quilts, silver, and furniture.

Simpson, Jeffrey. *The American Family: A History in Photographs.* **New York: Viking Press, 1976.**

Looking through this moving volume will inspire you to hunt for photos of your family and keep photos of yourself. They are an irreplaceable record of the past.

Diaries

Below are only two examples of many British diaries that have found their way into print, to give you some idea of the wealth of information they contain. These two give personal accounts of military service, which is invaluable to a family historian. When you've finished using any diary you find in your search, you might want to type it up so it can be shared with others.

> **Denham, H. M.** *Dardanelles: A Midshipman's Diary, 1915–16.* **London: Murray, 1981.**

> **Fairhead, R.** *An Airman's Diary.* **Great Britain: New Horizon, 1992.**

GRAVESTONES AND CEMETERIES

There are thousands of books that describe or index a specific graveyard or collection of cemeteries. Check for publications by the county where your ancestor is buried. If your library computer system allows it, search using the multiple key words "cemeteries" or "gravestones" plus the county name.

The American Cemetery. **Chicago: Prettyman Publishing.**

> This monthly has been around since the 1920s and continues to provide information on graveyards around the country, including historical landmarks and recent excavations.

The Association for Gravestone Studies
46 Plymouth Road
Needham, MA 02192

> Write to this association for a free brochure describing their publications about gravestones and cemeteries.

Bailey, Conrad. *Harrap's Guide to Famous London Graves.* **London: Harrap, 1975.**

> Illustrated with photographs, this is a fascinating guidebook, especially useful for a researcher who has traced roots to famous (and infamous) English people. Some mentioned here include monarchs, Sir Thomas More, and even Isaac Newton.

Jacobs, G. Walker. *Stranger Stop and Cast an Eye: A Guide to Gravestones and Gravestone Rubbing.* Brattleboro, VT: S. Greene Press, 1973.

Teaches how to do rubbings and what to look for on them. Words are not the only important aspect of stone etching; learn to recognize symbolism in the decorations. Illustrated with photos of rubbings from New England.

Jervise, Andrew. *Epitaphs and Inscriptions from Burial Grounds and Old Buildings in the Northeast of Scotland.* Edinburgh: Edmonston and Davglas, 1875–79.

This two-volume project offers valuable information collected from monuments in the Grampian and Highland areas of Scotland. The entries include vital statistics from gravestones, as well as the verses commemorating those buried there.

Kahn, Roy Max. *Gravestones of the United States, 1648–1850.* Berkeley, CA: Kahn, 1979.

Check this book to see if stones with the right surname are included in the photographed rubbings prepared by the author. There are very few copies of this book, so you will probably need to use interlibrary loan or visit a major research library.

Mitchell, John F., and Mitchell, Sheila. *List of Discovered Pre-1855 Grave Inscriptions.* Edinburgh: Scottish Genealogical Society, 1967–75.

This is an exhausive tally of cemetery rubbings from eleven counties in the Lowlands of Scotland: Kinrossshire, Clackmannanshire, West Lothian, Dunbartonshire, Renfrewshire, East Fife, West Fife, East Stirlingshire, West Stirlingshire, South Perthshire, and North Perthshire. Organized by location and indexed by surname.

Rodwell, Warwick. *The Archaeology of Religious Places: Churches and Cemeteries in Britain.* Philadelphia: University of Pennsylvania Press, 1989.

A history of excavations of old churches and their significance. Includes a good index and color illustrations. Archaeologists use grave markers to learn about changing religious rites or social conditions throughout prehistory and history.

Willsher, Betty, and Hunter, Doreen. *Stones: A Guide to Some Remarkable Eighteenth Century Gravestones.* **New York: Taplinger Publishing, 1979.**

The point of this book is to become familiar with the history of design and symbolism of Scottish monuments. A fascinating introduction to the subject, illustrated with photos from cemeteries all over Scotland.

Chapter 6
Documents and Libraries

Your grandmother's attic can be a treasure trove of exciting surprises and valuable information. The hints you get talking to your relatives will lead you in search of official documents. That does not mean that what you learn from your relatives is less important than what you find in print. You should keep a good record of every piece of information you collect, and exactly where you got it. Your relative's not-very-accurate memories of an ancestor in the military can be very valuable, since perhaps you didn't know that that ancestor had been in the military at all.

Once you do start looking in libraries and archives for documentation to corroborate your hunches, remember this: You can't always believe what you read.

Primary Sources

Don't worry, there are ways to tell the good sources from the questionable. Your best bet is always a class of documents known as "primary" because the writer of the document got his information firsthand, when the event occurred. Many primary sources are actually signed by the ancestor.

Birth and marriage certificates are great sources of reliable information about an ancestor. A birth certificate gives the baby's birth name, date and place of birth, weight, and parents' names. Vital records are also a source of clues to more information. If you make it as far back as three generations and then get stuck, hunt for birth and marriage certificates of the earliest known ancestor. They will show the name of at least one parent of that ancestor, giving you a window of opportunity to step back another generation. Write to the U.S. Government Printing Office for specific information on getting vital records from different periods of American history.

Land deeds and other contracts can shed light on a search. They give information about what real estate was owned or leased by the ancestor, when, and whether he or she lived there. Contracts involving your ancestor's work can offer clues about business connections and success. Wills show exactly what the ancestor owned in a certain year. They can also disclose the names of friends and relatives of the ancestor that you might not otherwise have run across.

Looking through old legal documents may sound fairly boring. Even for those of us who don't aspire to become lawyers, however, reading the last will and testament of an ancestor can be enlightening, heart-rending, or even funny:

> Whereas my eldest son . . . hath been extremely disobedient and undutifull unto me for these eighteen years past . . . and hath threatened to shorten my life, and hath hastily married his mother's chambermaid after having had an illegitimate child by her . . .
>
> —*Clues from English Archaeology: Contributory to American Genealogy.* J. H. Lea & J. R. Hutchinson, eds., Vol. 40, 1909, pp. 80–86.

This excerpt from a seventeenth-century British American's will proves that parents' becoming exasperated with their kids is not just a modern problem. Wills give clues about the ancestor's personality, allegiances, and, of course, property. Although it is rare, it does happen that a well-documented genealogy can prove that the researcher is an heir.

Death certificates and burial records should be used with great care. They are excellent primary sources for the place, date, and cause of death and the place of burial. The certificates include other information that cannot always be trusted, such as date and place of birth. The ancestor may have died far from his birthplace; coroners, not knowing any better, may have signed their names to inaccurate information.

Another way to document death information, especially

when certificates are lost or hard to find, is to visit grave-yards where your ancestors are buried. The cemeteries of America's east coast are teeming with British graves. Most of these graveyards have been indexed by the surnames of those who rest there. You can search for them at a library by look-ing up the county where you believe your ancestor is buried.

You can make a valuable document from a gravestone by putting a piece of paper over the words etched in the stone and rubbing it lightly with the side of a crayon or pencil. It takes some practice to get a clear rubbing of the name and dates on the stone. A firm hand holding the paper and a light touch with the crayon are good pointers to keep in mind. Be sure to mark on the back of each rubbing exactly where the stone lies.

When searching for primary records, it's always best to start with the county courthouse where you think the event took place. Write to the courthouse with a very specific query: Give the full name of the person, what documents you are seeking, and, if possible, the year in which the event occurred. Army records can be obtained from the federal government at the addresses at the end of this chapter. You will need to write to request a form, which you then fill out with specifics about the document you need. A small processing fee is charged for each document.

Hunting for Clues:
Genealogy Magazines and Societies

You may have no idea where or when an event took place. Then it is time to gather some more clues. Thousands of people in the United States are interested in genealogy. They subscribe to magazines about the subject and keep a lookout for anyone whose family lines might cross theirs. In the **Resources** sections of this book you will find many periodi-cals dealing with American and British American family history. Most public libraries subscribe to the most popular ones, such as *Everton's Genealogic Helper*. Ask your librarian for a few back issues of this one and others. They contain articles about general family history topics, such as heritage research problems, adoption searches, and book reviews.

You will find the pages packed with little classified ads: people are looking for other researchers who have information on a particular surname, a particular army regiment, or other clues. Skim through the ads. Some of them might involve your family. These people aren't selling anything; they don't want money. The commercial ads are easy to distinguish from requests for information. People heavily involved in genealogy act like a community, offering information when they have it and asking for help from their colleagues when they need it. They are always happy to welcome a new family historian. You might consider answering a query about one of your family surnames, letting somebody else know what you've found out.

Contacting the major American genealogy societies is a good idea for a beginner genealogist. Their addresses are given at the end of this chapter. Although there is a charge for membership, you will at least be able to get a catalog of publications without joining, and perhaps find out what research has already been done on your family lines.

Research Libraries

Eventually, as you become more involved in your search, your local public library will no longer serve your needs. You'll want to visit a research library. These are special collections, either publicly or privately owned, that are kept exclusively for researchers. You can't check books out, and usually you order the books you want, rather than going to a shelf and getting them. Don't worry, though, because there are plenty of people to help you. Just pack up some pencils and your family research binder, and don't forget to take along your pedigree chart.

Big libraries can be intimidating places, even for experienced researchers. Every time you go into a new library, there are new procedures to learn. If you are lucky enough to live near or visit a large research library to work on genealogy, keep in mind the most important resources it has to offer: its reference librarians.

A library may have the finest genealogy collection in the world, but it's useless to you if you don't know how to use it. Librarians have trained long and hard to be able to answer your specific questions about family history. They won't do your search for you, but they will be glad to give you advice. They'll show you the resources they have and teach you to use equipment or catalogs that are new to you. Don't be embarrassed to ask for help. And if you need help again later, ask some more questions.

As you embark on your research, remember that you are making an important record. When you get home from the library, you will be dependent on your own notes for all the information you got that day. Read carefully. Write clearly. Take down more information than you think you'll need. If the librarian will let you, photocopy pages that have a lot of information, especially if that information is in the form of names or numbers that are easy to copy down wrong. Don't mix the notes on one family group with those for another. Even if you end up with pages having only one or two sentences, it is much better to separate your notes by subject.

It is also very useful to keep a list of questions that occur to you as you research. You won't always be able to drop what you're doing and answer every question right then; writing them down allows you to deal with them later. Keep clear notes on where you got each piece of information. Include the book title, author, publisher, date, and page number. Also write down specifics on any source that was not helpful. That way you won't waste time accidentally going back to it on another day.

When you go to your school library, you probably look up a title, an author, or a subject in the card catalog, write down the call number, and go to the shelf for the book. It's not always quite so straightforward in genealogy. First, you've got to know what to look up. Where is the card catalog, anyway?

Ask a reference librarian. If it is your first trip to a research library for genealogy, the first question out of your mouth should be, "Could you please tell me how I can find out whether there is a published family history of the *(your ancestor's surname here)* family?"

A huge number of genealogists have written up as much of their family histories as they could piece together over years of research. Thousands of those researchers have actually published their written histories, and most of those have been catalogued and indexed. The particular library you go to may not have exactly the family history you need, but it may be out there somewhere.

OCLC and Interlibrary Loan

OCLC stands for Online Catalog of the Library of Congress. The nation's central library in Washington, DC, designed primarily to serve the needs of the U.S. Congress, is a vast resource for the general public as well. The catalog includes nearly everything published in the United States.

An important service offered by the Library of Congress is its computer catalog. Large research libraries will have access to this catalog (you'll probably need to ask for a librarian's permission to use it). If you enter your ancestor's surname as a subject, you may get lucky and come up with a published family history to help out your search. OCLC will also tell you which major libraries own the book.

If your ancestors established themselves on the east coast when they first arrived in America, but you live in another part of the country, you may find that your nearest research library doesn't have many books about the area that interests you. Through OCLC or bibliographies you can learn about books that may be of use. If the library at which you're doing research participates in an interlibrary loan program, it may be able to get you a book by ordering it from another library.

Interlibrary loan has limitations.

- Your library must have a loan agreement with the other library.
- The library that owns the book has the right to refuse to lend it. It may do so if the book is unique, rare,

damaged, or contains many removable pieces. Unfortunately, many published family histories fall into this category.

- Interlibrary loan is very expensive. Although you as a researcher are usually not asked to pay these costs, a library with a restricted budget may try to discourage you and may instead help you find a similar book in its own collection.

Indexes

If you are looking for specific information about a family line and can't find a published genealogy, talk to the reference librarian. He or she will ask you some questions, such as what period of time you're interested in and what city or part of the United States you believe your ancestor came to from Britain. Probably you will be directed to a computer, a set of books, or a microform projector to look at some sort of index to narrow down your search.

An index is a resource that tells you exactly where to look to find out about a certain subject. In genealogy, indexes are essential because the sources and documents are so numerous. Fortunately, scholars have culled them already. You will find indexes of ships' passenger lists. Look up your immigrant ancestor's last name, or the year or port of arrival, and you will find a list of places where the right passenger lists are published. Similar indexes exist for train passengers if you're tracing the movement of your ancestor across the American continent.

Governments publish registers and indexes of vital records, military service, and civil servants. They can tell you in what county or year events took place so you can request a copy of the official certificate from the event. Remember not to trust everything you read. Errors occur in registers and indexes, so it's best to look at the original document yourself once you've found out that it exists.

In Britain until 1837 vital records were kept by churches or synagogues, not by the central government. Known as "parish registers," these handwritten books of events were kept irregularly from the sixteenth century. Fortunately, they too have been indexed. Instead of having to write each county in Britain to find out where an ancestor was born, baptized, married, or buried, you can find all that information at the central register houses listed at the end of this chapter.

There are many indexes and catalogues of use to genealogists, including guides to biographies, land deeds, and rare manuscripts. There are also books to teach you how to make use of these resources for family history.

Censuses and the National Archives

Every ten years the federal government hires people to go from door to door all over the United States and find out who lives in each house. This practice has been going on in many parts of the world for thousands of years.

The information contained in a census is very valuable to a genealogist. You can learn your ancestors' first and middle names, the names of all their nuclear-family members, their addresses, ages, and some personal information. You can even see who in the household was deaf, dumb, blind, insane, a pauper (poor), or an ex-convict.

To protect privacy, the complete information from each census is sealed by the government in both the United States and Britain until most of the individuals who gave it have died. In 1992 the U.S. government released the 1920 census to the public. When these records become public, they are stored in the National Archives, a repository for outdated federal materials. You can visit the National Archives in Washington, DC, or one of its branches (listed at the end of this chapter) or use the censuses available from a large research library. It is also possible to order photocopies of certain census pages, or even buy or rent the microform of censuses for certain areas if you have enough use for it.

The United States began taking a census in 1790. Sadly, there was a serious fire at the National Archives in the early twentieth century, destroying most of the census records through 1880. The year 1890 survives only in fragments.

The loss of this irreplaceable information will always plague family historians.

The British house their censuses at the New Register House in Edinburgh, Scotland, and the General Register House in London, England. Their first national census was in 1841. It listed a person's name, address, and occupation; ages, however, were rounded down to the nearest half-decade (both a thirty-nine-year-old and a thirty-six-year-old would be reported as thirty-five). By 1851 the information became more detailed. To research the years before the national census began, a genealogist can turn to the Public Record Office in London. There you can find cess rolls, records from the seventeenth and eighteenth centuries registering the payment of taxes to fund military troops. Some rent and valuation rolls are available that show tenants' and landlords' names as well as a property's address and the dates it was occupied.

When you research the census in the United States, you choose a census year and check in the particular town census where you believe a relative lived that year. If you find ancestors in the census, take down all the information about them and their families. Even things that seem unimportant may prove useful at a later period of your research. If you're looking at the census of a small town, take down information on everyone with the correct surname, whether you're sure they're related or not. You can verify connections later.

As always, doubt what you see. People have a habit, even today, of not trusting census takers or the government. They have always tended to hide information or misrepresent some aspect of their household in the census, imagining that somehow it would keep trouble away. All it actually does is make research about the American population very difficult to do accurately. Always check the information you find against vital records.

Family History Library and Family History Centers

The largest genealogy library in the world is in Salt Lake

City, Utah. It is operated by The Church of Jesus Christ of Latter-day Saints (LDS), also known as the Mormons. The library's central purpose is religious: The Mormon belief system allows for people to be baptized after they die if they are found to be ancestors of living Mormons. The library was begun to trace the roots of Mormons all over the globe. Now it is a fundamental resource for genealogists of every religion and background.

The main library in Salt Lake City is called the Family History Library. Its holdings include microform versions of censuses, British parish registers, published family histories, vital records, historical gazetteers, and atlases. LDS scholars have spent years transcribing vital records from all over the world. The result is the International Genealogy Index (IGI), which holds the vital statistics on a staggering 150 million persons who died between 1500 and 1875.

The value of the LDS collection cannot be overstated. There is no better place to do British American genealogy research. It has been said that almost everyone with early American ancestry can find a family history prepared by LDS for at least one surname. Professional researchers have declared that preparing a British genealogy at the LDS is easier than doing it in Britain! Be aware, though, that the information in LDS sources is transcribed from original documents and occasionally contains errors.

Not everyone can get on a plane to Salt Lake City or stay there long enough to do much research. Fortunately, there are hundreds of regional branches of the main library, known as Family History Centers. Write to the main library at the address given in the reference section for the address of the Center nearest you.

The LDS also offers a general Family Registry. People looking for information about a certain family line can sign up there hoping for information from others on a similar search. Forms for placing or answering a query are available at Family History Centers.

Resources

INDEXES AND RESOURCE GUIDES

Armstrong, Norma S. *Local Collections in Scotland.* **Glasgow: Scottish Library Association, 1977.**

It is easy to find information on the holdings of major archives such as the New Register House in Edinburgh. This is a rare guide to smaller collections held in local libraries and historical societies all over Scotland. You can search the index by county or town.

A Catalogue of Parish Register Copies in the Possession of the Society of Genealogists. **London: Society of Genealogists, 1968.**

A look through this catalogue may help you decide whether to contact the Society of Genealogists for assistance in your search. They hold an archive of parish registers from all over Britain. The catalogue is organized by parish and date and indexed by surname.

A Catalogue of Welsh Manuscripts in the College of Arms. **London: Harleian Society, 1988.**

Well indexed and illustrated with maps and fascimiles of old documents, the College of Arms catalogue will show you some of the rare manuscripts that are available if your roots are Welsh. Especially important because it includes some unpublished family histories, in manuscript form.

A Collection of Genealogies of Families in the British Isles. **New York: New York Public Library, 1984.**

The New York Public Library Central Research Collection houses one of America's most extensive genealogy archives. These catalogs are useful both for visiting the library and for ordering through interlibrary loan. Some manuscripts are not available for loan because of their fragile condition. Check with your reference librarian.

Genealogical Periodical Annual Index. **Bowie, MD: Heritage Books.**

A large research library may have this extensive index on CD-ROM, which makes searching the 227 periodicals covered in it much more efficient. A paper version is also available.

The following are concise guides to documents in Britain. They include how to find the documents, how to request them from archives, how to use them, and how to apply the information they give you to your genealogical search.

Gibson, Jeremy, ed. *A Simplified Guide to Marriage, Census, and Other Indexes in Great Britain.* **Baltimore: Genealogical Publishing, 1986.**

An invaluable guide to the records you may depend on most when your research moves to Britain.

Holding, Norman H. *The Location of British Army Records.* **Solihull, England: Federation of Family History Societies, 1987.**

This book is important for the descendants of twentieth-century immigrants from Britain. It concentrates on record sources for British veterans of World War I.

Index Library of the British Record Society. **London: British Record Society.**

Since 1888 this index has been published and updated as a guide to legal and vital documents held in all parts of the United Kingdom.

Index to Personal Names in the National Union Catalog of Manuscript Collections 1959–1984. **Alexandria, VA: Chadwyck-Healy, Inc., 1988.**

Not comprehensive in its dates, but a helpful starting point when searching for family histories in NUCMUC (see below).

Iredale, David. *Enjoying Archives.* **Chichester, England: Phillimore, 1979.**

What a concept! Iredale uses wit and clarity to make the use of libraries and documents from Britain seem like child's play. He covers musuem collections and national registers and also gives tips for finding useful information in lawyers' files and relatives' attics.

Jackson, Ronald Vern. *Inventory of Church Records of the British Isles.* **Bountiful, UT: Accelerated Indexing Systems, 1976.**

Before the eighteenth century vital records of Britons were kept by the Church rather than the state. Jackson's *Inventory* can lead you to those records. It is a good place to check before writing to the Register House in London for similar information.

Moulton, Joy Wade. *Genealogical Resources in English Repositories.* **Columbus, OH: Hampton House, 1988.**

Especially useful to those who hope one day to visit Britain for family research, this comprehensive guide includes a description of many libraries and record offices, as well as maps showing where they are located.

National Index of Parish Registers. **London: Society of Genealogists, 1968–84.**

This twelve-volume set is difficult to find in the United States, but it is particularly useful if you are planning to do research in England. The LDS Family History Library has many English parish registers on microform for use in the United States.

National Union Catalog of Manuscript Collections. **Washington, DC: Library of Congress, 1991.**

Affectionately known as NUCMUC, this catalog will guide you to such useful rare manuscripts as handwritten family histories and other treasures that never reached publication. NUCMUC represents only a tiny percentage of such manuscripts, but at least it's a start.

Neagles, James C. *Confederate Research Sources: A Guide to Archive Collections.* **Salt Lake City: Ancestry Publishing, 1986.**

If you find or suspect that your British ancestors settled in the South, this book is a good resource to teach you how to learn more. It describes holdings, services, and specialties of each library.

Nikolic, Margaret. *Genealogical Microform Holdings in Scottish Libraries.* **Kirkcaldy, Scotland: Kirkcaldy District Council, 1992.**

If you have the opportunity to do research in Scotland, this book will be an invaluable timesaver. You can decide what you need and which libraries it will be most efficient to visit. You can also write ahead and reserve material in advance.

Owen, Dolores B. *Guide to Genealogical Resources in the British Isles.* **Metuchen, NJ: Scarecrow Press, 1989.**

Public and private libraries as well as special archives are covered in this thorough directory. Describes the holdings, lending policies, photocopying and search services, and locations of important archives all over Britain.

Pope, Wiley R. *A Checklist of English Genealogical and Historical Works at the Minnesota Historical Society Reference Library.* **St. Paul: Minnesota Family Trees, 1982.**

The genealogy search group Minnesota Family Trees put out this helpful volume. The library's collection includes sources from England as well as information on British families that settled in the Midwest.

Thomson, Theodore Radford. *A Catalogue of British Family Histories.* **London: Research Publishing, for the Society of Genealogists, 1976.**

Although by no means complete, this catalogue may prove useful for finding rare information on family lines that you have traced back to Britain.

DOCUMENTS AND GUIDES FOR USING THEM

Alcock, N.W. *Old Title Deeds: A Guide for Local and Family Historians.* Chichester, England: Phillimore, 1986.

A short introduction to land titles and deeds in Britain and how they are useful to the genealogist. It includes a guide to Latin terms and abbreviations that occur frequently in *seizin* documents.

Beers, Henry Putney. *The Confederacy: A Guide to the Archives of the Confederate States of America.* Washington, DC: National Archives, 1986.

The National Archives is one of the best sources for both historical and genealogic information concerning the South during the Civil War. This book guides you in the use of records involving the military, the government, trade, and civilians.

Boreham, John. *The Census and How to Use It.* Brentwood, England: Essex Society for Family History, 1983.

A concise introduction to using British censuses. It explains in step-by-step instructions how each census is laid out, what information it contains, and how to use it. Usually available on microfilm in American libraries.

Bureau of the Census
Pittsburg, KS 66762

This is where you write for information on censuses not yet released to the public (since 1920). They'll send you a form and a list of fees.

Civilian Personnel Records
111 Winnebago Street
St. Louis, MO 63118

Write here for an order form for information on civilian employees of the U.S. government after 1909.

Colwell, Stella. *Dictionary of Genealogical Sources in the Public Record Office.* London: Weidenfeld & Nicolson, 1992.

————. *Family Roots: Discovering the Past in the Public Record Office*. London: Weidenfield & Nicolson, 1991.

Stella Colwell has published extensively as a spokesperson for the Public Record Office in London. She offers clear, thorough guides to its resources. The *Dictionary* is an alphabetical listing of source by type and family name, and *Family Roots* is a how-to research manual.

Dollarhide, William, and Thorndale, William. *Map Guide to the U.S. Federal Censuses, 1790–1920*. **Baltimore: Genealogical Publishing, 1987.**

This guide shows what areas are covered in surviving censuses. Very useful if you know the general area but not the exact town where an ancestor lived.

The East India Company
If you find that some of your ancestors were involved in the British imperialization of India, you will be pleased to learn that most records of interest to genealogists have been collected and published. Here is a sampling. The following volumes were complied and edited by Edward Dodwell and James Samuel Miles in 1839.

> *East India Company's Bengal Civil Servants, 1780–1838.*
>
> *East India Company's Bombay Civil Servants, 1794–1839.*
>
> *East India Company's Madras Civil Servants, 1780–1839.*
>
> *Medical Officers of the Indian Army, 1764–1838.*
>
> *Officers of the Indian Army, 1760–Sept. 30, 1837.*

Fowler, Simon. *Army Records for the Family Historian*. **London: Public Record Office, 1982.**

This book, produced by one of the biggest document repositories in Britain, offers tips for applying their holdings to your genealogical search. Learn what to look for and how to request it when you're searching for an ancestor who served in the British Army.

Gibson, Jeremy Sumner Wycherly. *Probate Jurisdiction: Where to Look for Wills,* 3rd ed. Baltimore: Genealogical Publishing, 1989.

When tracing testaments in Britain, you will find that laws and repository customs differ from those in the United States. This book explains it all clearly. Includes maps.

A Guide to Genealogical Sources in Guildhall Library. London: Corporation of London, 1979.

Guildhall Library is a major genealogical source in London. This book lists the library's strengths and gives you directions for requesting minimal searches by mail.

Hamilton-Edwards, Gerald. *In Search of Army Ancestry.* London: Phillimore, 1977.

If you are seeking information about a relative with army connections, Hamilton-Edwards will guide your search through the United Kingdom, complete with amusing cartoons.

Immigration and Naturalization Service Washington, DC 20536

Naturalization records after 1906 are available here. Write for an order form.

Kaminkow, Marion J. *Genealogies in the Library of Congress: A Bibliography.* Baltimore: Magna Carta, 1972.

There is no better introduction to the family histories available in the Library of Congress than this two-volume work.

———. *A Complement to Genealogies in the Library of Congress.* Baltimore: Magna Carta, 1981.

Kaminkow strikes again, providing an essential update to the Library of Congress collection.

Kitzmiller, John M. *In Search of the "Forlorn Hope": A Comprehensive Guide to Locating British Regiments and Their Records (1640–WWI).* Salt Lake City: Manuscript Publishing Foundation, 1988.

The advantage of this set of two thick volumes is that it offers advice on searching in the United States for British Army troops and officers. It gives an introduction to the military system in Britain and specific instructions for ordering information about your ancestor.

Markwell, F. C. *Facsimile Documents of Use to Family Historians.* Solihull, U.K.: Federation of Family History Societies, 1987.

Facsimile is a technique of copying rare, often handwritten material. Using this material can be a fascinating adventure, but it can be difficult to find and decipher. Markwell gives advice on which kinds of British documents to look for in facsimile.

Matriculation Rolls

Since their inception, universities have kept records of every student they have enrolled. Especially for the centuries before British record keeping became centralized, checking university records can offer valuable information.

Graduation and Matriculation Rolls of the University of St. Andrews, 1413–1897.

Mackie, John Duncan. The University of Glasgow, 1451–1951.

Oxford University Rolls of Graduation, 1300–1900.

The University of Aberdeen Rolls of Graduates, 1495–1925.

Military Personnel Records
9700 Page Boulevard
St. Louis, MO 63132

Ask for Standard Form 180, "Request Pertaining to Military Records" for information on the Army (after 1912), Navy (after 1885), or Marines (after 1895).

Munden, Kenneth W., and Beers, Henry Putney. *The Union: A Guide to Federal Archives Relating to the Civil War.* Washington, DC: National Archives, 1986.

A companion volume to Beers' *The Confederacy*, concentrating on those families who settled in the Yankee states.

National Archives
General Reference Branch (NNRG)
Washington DC 20048

Write for forms needed to order photocopies of specific pages of a census.

National Archives Trust Fund (NEPS)
P.O. Box 100793
Atlanta, GA 30384

Write here to inquire about purchasing particularly useful censuses on microform and CD-ROM.

Parker, J. Carlyle. *Going to Salt Lake City to Do Family History Research*. Turlock, CA: Marietta Publishing, 1989.

The central Family History Library can be an overwhelming place if you're not prepared. This guide offers advice on organizing and focusing your search before you go.

Passport Office
State Department
Washington, DC 20520

Write here for passport applications after 1926.

Raymond, Stuart A. *Occupational Sources for Genealogists: A Bibliography*. Birmingham: Federation of Family History Societies, 1992.

A great deal can be learned by checking documents having to do with an ancestor's work, whether he was a schoolteacher or a miner. The author offers a list of sources in Britain.

Rogers, Barbara. *An Intermediate Guide to Salt Lake City Library English Research Sources*. Vancouver, Canada: British Columbia Genealogical Society, 1984.

When you've visited your nearest Family History Library

branch and have a good idea of how its system works, see Rogers's book for more specific information on British searches.

LIBRARIES

Family History Library (FHL)
35 North West Temple Street
Salt Lake City, UT 84150

Affiliated with The Church of Jesus Christ of Latter-day Saints, this is the largest genealogical library in the world. Besides having compiled a staggering collection of information, FHL has long been at the forefront of genealogical research technology. Everything from American censuses to parish registers from Wales can be ordered on microfilm and, increasingly, on CD. Family History Library has branches all over the world, staffed by volunteers. A trip to the central Utah Library is quite a treat if you can manage it, but FHL strongly recommends that you visit your nearest branch first.

National Archives and Records Administration
Washington, DC 20408

Write for free catalogs of their publications and microfilms. This is the storehouse for censuses, vital records, and many other documents essential to genealogists. Some National Archives free publications: *Military Service Records in the National Archives*; *Using Records in National Archives for Genealogical Research*; *Getting Started Beginning Your Genealogical Research in the National Archives*.

National Archives Regional Archives
Central Plains
2312 East Bannister Road
Kansas City, MO 64131
816-926-6272

Information on Iowa, Kansas, Missouri, Nebraska.

Great Lakes
7358 South Pulaski Road
Chicago, IL 60629
312-581-7816

Information on Illinois, Indiana, Michigan, Minnesota, Ohio, Wisconsin.

Mid-Atlantic
Ninth and Market Streets
Philadelphia, PA 19107
215-597-3000

Information on Delaware, Maryland, Pennsylvania, Virginia, West Virginia.

New England
380 Trapelo Road
Waltham, MA 02154
617-647-8100

Information on Connecticut, Maine, Massachusetts, New Hampshire, Rhode Island, Vermont.

Northeast
Building 22—MOT Bayonne
Bayonne, NJ 07002-5388
201-823-7252

Information on New Jersey, New York, Puerto Rico, Virgin Islands.

Pacific Northwest
6125 Sand Point Way NE
Seattle, WA 98115
206-526-6507

Information on Alaska, Idaho, Oregon, Washington state.

Pacific Sierra
1000 Commodore Drive
San Bruno, CA 94066
415-876-9009

Information on Hawaii, Nevada, northern California.

Pacific Southwest
24000 Avila Road
Mailing Address: P.O. Box 6719
Laguna Niguel, CA 92677-6719
714-643-4241

Information on Arizona, southern California, Nevada's Clark County.

Rocky Mountain
Building 48, Denver Federal Center
Denver, CO 80225
303-236-0818

Information on Colorado, Montana, North Dakota, South Dakota, Utah, Wyoming.

Southwest
501 West Felix Street
Mailing address: P.O. Box 6216
Fort Worth, TX 76115
817-334-5525

Information on Arkansas, Louisiana, New Mexico, Oklahoma, Texas.

Chapter 7
The Idea of Lineage

I am an Englishman by my birth and Marlborough
is my name.
In Devonshire I drew my breath, that place of
noted fame.
I was beloved by all my men, by kings and princes
likewise;
And many towns I often took, and I did the world
surprise.

Family lines have long meant more than just what people
you were related to and what ethnic and religious background was yours. The idea behind pedigrees was to keep
track of who owned what property or belonged to which
trade guild. The landed gentry—those people to whom the
monarchs of Britain had granted land—passed their property
to their children. If a nobleman had no living children, the
legitimate heir had to be found from among other family
members. There developed customs of naming people so
that their family ties would be obvious. Learning a little
about these conventions can open a researcher to clues in
British genealogy.

Names

Long ago in Britain people were given one name only.
Through the Middle Ages, these names usually came from
the New Testament of the Christian Bible. Parish priests,
who were responsible for keeping vital records for their con-
gregation, ran into confusion. There might be fifteen men
named John in any given parish. The priests began distin-
guishing the many identically named parishioners by where

they lived or what they did for a living. Attwater is a surviving example (at-the-water's edge), as are the names Rivers and Mill. Smith is still the most common last surname in Britain, dating from a period when metalworkers were named after their trade. Nicknames such as Stout, Short, and Reid (redhead) sometimes caught on as surnames.

Patronymics, names based on a person's father's name, became the vogue as administrators pushed surnames into popularity. In Scots-Gaelic, *mac* means "son." The Scots also joined the English in tacking the word "-son" to the father's name. Robert MacDonald is Robert, son of Donald. The names used to change with every generation, however, based on the father's name. Robert MacDonald's son Peter would be named Peter Robertson, not Peter MacDonald. Understanding that concept can help you use parish registers from Scotland.

The traditional Scots were fairly predictable in naming. The eldest son was almost always named after his paternal grandfather, and the eldest daughter after her mother's mother. The second son would be named after his maternal grandmother, and the third son after his father. Watch out, though: Because infant mortality rates were so high, it was common for a family to give two siblings the same name, in case one of them died!

Parts of ancient Scotland had a matrilineal culture, meaning that property was passed down through a woman's direct family line, rather than her husband's. A reminder of this is the fact that into the seventeenth century some women did not take their husband's name when they married.

Patronymics were the most popular kind of surname in Wales beginning in the sixteenth century. Like the Scots and English, they used their native word for "son" in the name. *Ab* or *ap* would be inserted between the son's and father's names: John ap Richard was John, son of Richard. They didn't stop there, though. Proud of their family lines, they would hold onto previous generations' patronymics in their own name. Even into the nineteenth century it was possible to find persons sporting three or four surnames tied together with *ab* or *ap*. As surnames became standardized, traces of the word for "son" sometimes remained. The names "Powell" and "Parry" are shortened forms of the Welsh patronymics "ap Howell" and "ap Harry."

A widespread English settlement of Wales began in the twelfth century; thus many names that may sound English are associated primarily with Wales. Amid the obviously Welsh surnames like Dafydd and Gwillym, you will commonly find Edwards, Roberts, and Williams.

Many names that were originally Gaelic have lost their native Scottish character. A name that began as MacGhillemhiure has changed into forms like Morison and Gilmore. Influences from as far back as the eleventh century still affect names in Britain, when the Normans contributed the prefixes *Fitz-* and *de-*, and the Scandinavians left the suffix *-sen*. Some names, also, were changed by the crossing of the Atlantic. Secretaries of shipping companies when making up passenger lists and customs officials registering new immigrants to America often misheard a name or spelled it phonetically. Many of the workers who immigrated to America were illiterate, so they didn't know that their name had been altered.

Clans

All of ancient Scotland was divided into clans, or groups of families who followed one leader. The system had died out in the Lowlands by 1300 when English influence became strong, but the Highlanders and Island dwellers held fast to their Gaelic clans for several more centuries. (The Scottish Highlands and Lowlands are divided by Scotland's Grampian Mountains.) The most powerful clan was the Campbells, who ruled the Western Highlands. Not every Campbell today is related to every other by blood, but each is descended from a family affiliated with the Campbell clan.

Clan families adopted the name of their leader, or chieftain. Belonging to a powerful clan offered protection and security in the rough environment of northern Scotland, where food was difficult to grow and no central government

Scottish clans often went to war over scarce resources. Clans were groups of families under single leadership.

kept warfare and raiding under control. On the other side of the coin, chieftains were interested in gaining new families for their clan, to make their fighting forces stronger. A chieftain would make offers of grain or other valuables to poor families to lure them under his protection and command. Some of these families would then adopt the leader's name, but with a variation to show that they weren't "the real MacCoy," as the saying goes. In the Middle Ages it became less popular for a new family joining a clan to adopt the clan's name. Instead, their own surname line would be known as a *sept* of the clan they joined.

In your research you may run into some unusual or repetitive Scottish names. Macdonald of Macdonald designates the chieftain of the Macdonald clan. By the nineteenth century, the chieftain title "Macdonald of that Ilk" was common, meaning "the very same Macdonald who gave his name to that people."

As industrialization changed the face of the British economy, even the ancient highland clans began to disperse. Young Scots sought work in the cities of Britain and continental Europe or took off for the United States. It was because of this scattering of clan members that clan associations began to be formed. In that way, clan ties can still be celebrated even when members are spread all over the world. These associations publish newsletters in Britain and hold annual clan meetings at which anyone with genealogical ties to the group may participate. Similar societies have sprung up in the United States to keep Scottish Americans in touch with their clan roots. If you are of Scottish descent and would like to learn about your clan, you will find some useful addresses at the end of this chapter.

Nobility

In medieval times a system was established that allowed the ruling monarch of Britain to give pieces of land to certain people in his or her royal favor. These pieces of land are known as peerages. Peers, then are "landed gentry," or aristocrats who own land through a gift of the King or

The miserable conditions of Britain's industrial revolution provided incentive for many working people to leave for America.

Queen. A peerage stays in the chosen noble family as long as there are blood ties left to claim it. You can see how important genealogy is to British nobility. If no provable kin comes forward, a peerage will go into "dormancy." Occasionally a thorough genealogical search will unearth an heir to a dormant peerage, often of British American stock.

The terminology associated with nobility and land titles in Britain can make a genealogist's head spin. Here are some basic pointers.

There are five classes of peerages in England, Scotland, and Wales. They are arranged in a ladder of increasing importance, called a squirearchy. The terms for the squirearchy and its squires, from top to bottom, are: 1) a duke in a dukedom (or duchy), 2) a marquise in a marquisate, 3) an earl in an earldom, 4) a viscount in a viscounty, and 5) a baron in a barony. (Try not to confuse barony and baronage; the latter refers to all the land granted to all the peers combined.)

As if this weren't enough, in the seventeenth century the King of England added another kind of peerage, called a baronetcy (owned by a baronet). There are no baronetcies within the boundaries of England, Scotland, or Wales. Instead, they were designed as bribes to persuade British noblemen to settle in Nova Scotia, Canada, and Ulster, Northern Ireland. Many people accepted these peerages, but most got around having to travel to what they considered "barbaric" countries: They would have a box of earth from their baronetcy shipped overseas to them in England, so that they could sign all the proper legal documents while standing on the soil of their granted land, as required by law.

As you can see in the verse from a traditional song about the Duke of Marlborough that begins this chapter, nobility were (and are) referred to by the name of their estate. In early legal documents they even signed their estate name instead of their personal name. Fortunately for family historians, this cryptic practice went out of style. In documents after 1672 you will find that the gentry sign their full name, followed by their title: "John Smith, Earl of Gloucester."

There is no question that tracing noble lineage is easier than tracing the roots of commoners, especially once your search has reached back to Britain. Because the future of a peerage depended on keeping track of potential heirs, writing down the pedigree of every member of nobility was a governmental concern. There are countless volumes of books holding nothing but family histories of the British aristocracy. No need to wade through parish registers to find out information about your ancestor the Duke.

If you need more information, or confirmation that your ancestor was noble, the Sasine Register reaches back into the fifteenth century and follows the granting of land in every peerage of the crown. The word *sasine* is an early Scots version of the English word *seizin*, related to the modern word "seize." It refers to the annexation of a piece of land to someone's personal property. Turn to the Service of Heirs to learn who inherited what since 1437. The Register of Deeds is considered one of the most valuable records for Scottish genealogy. It contains centuries' worth of contracts for purchasing a business, ordering a castle to be built, having a bog drained, hiring an apprentice, and other legal activities that might occupy a nobleman's energies.

Nobility in Scotland and Wales

Since 1707 in the case of Scotland and the mid-sixteenth century for Wales, the peerage has all been one big system under the central control of Great Britain. Before those marks in history, nobility in England, Scotland, and Wales were managed separately.

The original Welsh landed gentry dated from the fourteenth century. At that time Anglo-Norman families who had settled in Wales generations before established estates for themselves to rule over the surrounding native Celts. Over the centuries, the Normans blended culturally with the indigenous people, and the nobility likewise blended to a degree with commoners. What sets early Welsh nobility apart from its later English form is the egalitarian relationship between a lord and his servants. The rugged Welsh countryside was no place to get wealthy, and a nobleman had to get out and work alongside his farmhands just to make ends meet. Nevertheless, this order of aristocracy was respected by the common people for its noble lineage. The Welsh people called them *Yr Uchelwyr*, "the high ones."

In the sixteenth century, England began intensive settlement of Welsh lands. Original noble families were conveniently disposed of, because in the changing political climate, it was not hard to convict anyone of "treason" who was in your way. Once the incumbent nobleman was hanged for resisting the new regime, his land would be granted to a new family of the King's choosing. Soon all of Wales had been granted to peers in the English system. Today, Wales is still considered the principality of the King or Queen of England's son. The heir to the British crown is called the Prince of Wales.

Most of Scotland's peerages were established before the administrative merger with England in 1707. Those original Scottish peerages have been meticulously documented since their inception. *The Scots Peerage,* a nine-volume treasure chest of family history information, includes every pre-1707 land grant, as well as tracing the inheritance of that property to the present day.

The Scots use two titles that are not part of the English peerage system. The first is *Laird.* From the English word "lord," this title refers to a person named "tenant in chief" of a piece of land on behalf of the Crown of Scotland. The title *master* in Scotland officially refers to the heir apparent of an estate.

Coats of Arms

During the Crusades in twelfth-century Europe, knights roamed the hills seeking warfare and adventure. To identify themselves, they designed emblems that they wore into battle on their shields and banners. These emblems were stylized drawings of weapons and symbols to show aspects of the knight's family of origin.

Over time the symbols used for knights' identifying emblems were codified into a system that could communicate a great deal about the bearer's noble line. Placed atop a warrior's helmet, the coats of arms became a way to recognize a friend in the confusion of the battlefield. It also became a mark of aristocracy.

The development of coats of arms went unchecked in England for a century. At last there were so many insignia that certain people made a living just learning every nobleman's coat of arms and recognizing the arms borne by a party approaching the castle or army camp. These experts were called heralds, and coats of arms came to be known as heraldry.

By the early fifteenth century, King Henry V of England officially acknowledged that the heraldry craze had gotten out of hand. Everyone with any noble blood was wearing a crest, and new designs were appearing at every turn. They no longer served as identification; they had become more of a fashion statement. Henry instructed his heralds to develop strict rules governing both how a coat of arms could be designed and who was allowed to wear it.

Heraldry is an enormous and fascinating subject, and many fine books are listed at the end of this chapter to give you a detailed look at its history and artistry. You may be wondering, however, what it has to do with genealogy.

Just like noble or royal blood, an affiliation with a coat of arms passes from one generation to the next, no matter how many centuries or miles are between you and the original ancestor who wore it. Not everyone who is related to a noble family has the right to wear that family's coat of arms.

A person who has a right to bear the family emblem is called an armiger. This person must be descended from the eldest son of the eldest son of the original armiger knight. Because so many noble British families took up residence in America, it does happen that British Americans find themselves entitled to arms. Descendants of second sons of the noble line may be eligible for a specially designed emblem called "differenced arms," based on the family's true coat of arms.

Genealogy magazines are full of offers to send you "your official coat of arms." Don't believe them. There are only two officials with the power to endow you with your arms. In England that person is called the Earl Marshal, and in Scotland he is the Lord Lyon. These are the top heralds, and any claim to noble lineage must be authenticated through them, just as it has been since the early fifteenth century.

The addresses for the Earl Marshal and Lord Lyon are listed in the following reference section. You should write to them if you find that you have at least one noble family line. They will advise you whether you are entitled to a coat of arms. You may not have a helmet or shield to put it on, but a heraldic crest makes a stunning illustration for the first page of a family history.

Resources

TITLES AND NOBLE LINEAGE

Addington, Arthur Charles. *The Royal House of Stuart: The Descendants of King James VI of Scotland, James I of England.* **London: Skilton, 1969.**

James I, son of the Scottish Queen Mary Stuart, ruled England from 1603 to 1625. You can search by surname to learn whether you have Jacobite roots. Many of these descendants found their lives cut short by the radically shifting political climate.

Charles-Edwards, T. M. *Early Irish and Welsh Kinship.* **New York: Oxford University Press, 1993.**

For advanced readers interested in exploring kinship. A study of traditional Celtic kinship patterns (based on clans) up to AD 1500. The author demonstrates how those traditions changed under the influence of English settlers in Ireland and Wales.

Douglas, Sir Robert, and Wook, John Philip. *The Peerage of Scotland,* **2 vols. Conway, AR: Oldbuck Press, 1993.**

This is a reissue of the 1813 documentation of the history and genealogy of thousands of Scottish families, not all of them noble. Includes engravings of families' coats of arms.

The Genealogist's Guide. **London: Research Publishing, 1977.**

An index to printed British pedigrees and family histories. The first of three volumes was begun in the late nineteenth century by George William Marshall, the second prepared by John Beach Whitome, and the third—which includes histories printed up to 1975—is by Geoffrey Barrow.

Goldham, Peter Wilson. *American Loyalist Claims.* **Washington, DC: National Genealogical Society, 1980.**

Information from the British Public Record Office about colonists who remained loyal to the Crown of England and made claims to property in America. Some of these people returned to England after the revolution, while some fled to the strongly Anglo Canada.

Hotten, John. *The Original List of Persons of Quality Who Went from Great Britain to the American Plantations, 1600–1700.* **Baltimore: Genealogical Publishing, 1962.**

If you're searching for a line of nobility that emigrated to the Southern states, this may be helpful. It is mostly passenger lists from ships landing in Baltimore. You can search its index by surname.

Nicholas, Thomas. *Annals and Antiquities of the Counties and County Families of Wales.* **Baltimore: Genealogical Publishing, 1991.**

The reissue of nineteenth-century papers on the ranks, lineage, alliances, ensigns, residences, and ancient pedigrees of Wales' landed gentry. It focuses on the newer British-Welsh noble families but does include more ancient Norman-Welsh lines if they were still in possession of land at the time.

Roberts, Gary Boyd. *American Ancestors and Cousins of the Princess of Wales.* **Baltimore: Genealogical Publishing, 1984.**

Now you can finally find out whether Princess Di is any kin of yours. Some of her forebears settled in New England, on the mid-Atlantic coast, and in Virginia. Check your surname in the index.

———. *The Royal Descents of 500 Immigrants to the American Colonies or the United States.* **Baltimore: Genealogical Publishing, 1993.**

Roberts concentrates on those immigrants and their descendants who made a notable contribution to American history. They include politicians in particular, and some theologians and important traders.

Sheppard, Walter Lee. *Feudal Genealogy*. Washington: National Genealogical Society, 1975.

In the Middle Ages all of Britain was organized according to the feudal system. That system continued among the clans of the Scottish Highlands into the seventeenth century. This book discusses the strict hierarchy of that structure and what records were kept on each level of society.

Stevenson, Noel C. *Genealogical Evidence: A Guide to the Standard of Proof Relating to Pedigrees, Ancestry, Heirship and Family History*, rev. ed. Laguna Hills, CA: Aegean Park Press, 1989.

If your genealogical research leads you to believe that you stand a chance of inheriting a million bucks or being crowned prince of the Hebrides, be sure to consult this book first. It shows you all the sources you need to check before making a claim, and then whom to clear your claim with.

Taute, Anne. *Kings and Queens of Great Britain*. New York: Viking Penguin, 1990.

Not so much a book as a chart, this lavishly illustrated pedigree table shows a thorough royal genealogy of Britain, complete with coats of arms.

HERALDRY

To find out whether you have a right to bear a British coat of arms, you must contact for official documentation:

**Secretary to the Earl Marshal
The College of Arms
Queen Victoria Street
London EC4V 4BT**

If you simply want to find out what arms your ancestors wore, you should write with a specific request to the:

**Heraldry Society
28 Museum Street
London WC1A 1LH**

For crests established before 1707 in Scotland, a separate legislative body exists. The laws are much stricter governing the use of crests. Wearing a false crest in Scotland can land you in jail. Also different from England is the fact that women can be armigers in Scotland if they are the first in birth in the correct line. Contact:

**Court of the Lord Lyon
Lyon Office
HM New Register House
Edinburgh EH1 3YT**

Allcock, Hubert. *Heraldic Design*. New York: Tudor Publishing, 1962.

A straightforward description of what is contained in coats of arms and how they came to be that way.

Chorzempa, Rosemary A. *Design Your Own Coat of Arms*. New York: Dover, 1987.

Brief, with large illustrations, this book explains many of the devices used to make a family crest. If you follow the instructions, understand that you will not be making an official coat of arms. It is fascinating, though, to work with the symbols until they mean something to you.

Filby, P. William. *American and British Genealogy and Heraldry*. Chicago: American Library Association, 1983.

If you want to delve deeply into the subject of coats of arms and lineages, this huge bibliography is a good place to start. You may find a publication focusing on a surname to which you are linked.

Friar, Stephen. *Heraldry for the Local Historian and Genealogist*. Wolfeboro Falls, NH: Alan Sutton, 1992.

Written specifically as an aid to family historians tracing British roots. The book teaches how to recognize coats of arms for particular areas and surnames, and where to look for heraldic seals among documents and artifacts.

SCOTTISH CLANS AND TARTANS

**Council of Scottish Clan Associations, Inc.
7 Wyndmoor Drive
Convent Station, NJ 07961**

Your source for Scottish clan meetings, festivals, and family line information in the United States. Publishes a quarterly newletter, *The Claymore.*

MacDonald, Micheil. *Clans of Scotland.* Conway, AR: Oldbuck Press, 1993.

A short introduction to the fascinating and powerful clan system that ruled the highlands of Scotland for over a thousand years. Color illustrations.

Pine, Leslie Gilbert. *The Highland Clans.* Newton, U.K.: Abbot, David and Charles, 1972.

Were your ancestors highwaymen or blacksmiths? Famous warriors or infamous thieves? A general background on clans, organized by name and region.

———. *Tartan: The Highland Textile.* London: Shepheard-Walwyn, 1990.

An unusual look at tartans, focusing on their practical creation. Considers the weaving of tartan patterns as a tra-ditional Scottish handicraft, and the development of those patterns as the creativity of weavers. Includes interesting information on spinning, dyeing, and weaving techniques.

Scottish Tartans Society. *The Guide to Scottish Tartans.* London: Shepheard-Walwyn, 1977.

The key to learning the Scottish clans is to recognize tartans. This book matches tartans with their families and history. Includes indexes and a Scots-English glossary.

BRITISH GENEALOGICAL SOCIETIES SOURCES

England/Great Britain
Federation of Family Historical Societies
Administrator
31 Seven Star Road
Sollihul, West Midlands B91 2BZ

This remarkable organization is a sort of headquarters and clearinghouse for almost all family history activity in the British Isles. Publishes a quarterly journal, *Family History News and Digest*, plus occasional books and papers.

Local History Societies in England and Wales: A List.
London: Standing Conference for Local History.

Local history is a little different from family history. Instead of tracing the movement of a particular family to many places, it concentrates on one place and records what families moved in and out.

The London and Middlesex Genealogical Directory.
Ilford, Essex: Association of London and Middlesex Family History Societies.

Updated periodically, this directory will lead you to specific organizations and resources in the town or region from which your ancestors came. You may find that a researcher there is already involved in a project concerning your surname.

Society of Genealogists
14 Charterhouse Building
London EC1

This group publishes many books, pamphlets, and indexes, invaluable guides for doing research using British sources. Write for a list of publications and membership information.

Scotland
National Library of Scotland
George IV Building
Edinburgh 1

Scots Ancestry Research Society
3 Albany Street
Edinburgh EH1 3PY

Scottish Genealogical Society
Honorable Secretary
21 Howard Place
Edinburgh EH3 5JY

Scottish Tartans Society
Davidson House
Drummond Street
Comrie, Crieff
Perthshire

Wales

The Honorable Society of Cymrodorion
118 Newgate Street
London EC1A 7AE

An association of Welsh family historians in England.

National Library of Wales
Aberystwyth SY23 3BU

Write for information on their family history collection.

Registrar General of Shipping and Seamen
Llantrisant Road
Llandff
Cardiff CF5 2YS

Write with specific queries regarding sailors and merchant mariners.

University College of North Wales Library
Department of Manuscripts
Bangor
Gwynedd LL57 2DG

Write for information about rare family and local history manuscripts.

Chapter 8
Preserving What You Find

You've interviewed your relatives, collected vital documents, and spent some time at the library. All that work, and what have you got? A big pile of notes.

"Oh, thanks a lot," you're thinking. "What am I supposed to do with all this stuff?"

But now comes the part that can be the most fun. You get to combine your well-honed skills as a detective with the creativity of a writer and artist. It's time to make a family tree and start writing your family history.

Family Tree

A family tree can be anything from a piece of notebook paper showing a simple chart of your family to a big, elaborate wall decoration.

The idea is to have the trunk represent a particular ancestor (perhaps the original immigrant ancestor who came from Britain). His children, grandchildren, and the following generations and marriages are the branches. You may have been able to find information for many branches, or for only a few. The trunk ancestor should be the earliest kin for whom you have certain information.

The best way to begin is by finding out exactly what is in that big heap of notes. Go through it page by page. Make sure everything that has to do with a certain family group is in that group's file folder, not floating around without a home. Compare your notes with the pedigree chart that you've been filling out as you did research. Your pedigree chart probably will not be complete, but that doesn't matter. Be sure that all of the vital statistics that you have proof of appear on your pedigree chart.

Each entry on the tree should include the person's name, birth date, birth place, marriage date, death date, and burial place. If you are missing some of this information, by all means put the person on the tree anyway. You can always fill in the blanks later. If you are missing entire people (for example, you know that one of your ancestors was married but you couldn't find any information on the spouse), leave blank lines in the appropriate spot on the tree. If you have traced more than one surname, you can make a separate tree for each.

It is fun to make your family tree look like an actual tree. Trees are not the easiest things to draw, however. If your skills are stronger as a genealogist than as an artist, perhaps a friend or relative can help you out. It is also possible to buy preprinted, blank family trees from genealogy supply companies. If you were lucky enough to find any photographs of your relatives, you might want to use them to illustrate your tree. Make photocopies of the pictures and cut out squares that include the face of each person. Glue each person's face on the tree above his or her name.

Oral History

A family tree represents only the bare bones of the work you must do to trace your pedigree. Sure, you have been careful to obtain vital statistics on everyone, which is central to a successful genealogy project. But along the way you have picked up all kinds of interesting information that doesn't go on the tree.

When you interviewed your relatives at the beginning of your search, they told you stories. As you taped their words, they were giving you a priceless gift whether they knew it or not. Those family legends, or personal memories about a certain ancestor, add up to your family's oral history. These are anecdotes, usually unprovable, that are passed from generation to generation. Tales can be based on real events but become exaggerated for effect or altered by the intervening years. Your grandmother might tell you a story that supposedly happened to her grandfather when he was a boy.

Your grandmother hadn't even been born yet, so she doesn't know how much of it is true. It's a good story, though, and emphasizes a personal characteristic that she remembers in her grandfather.

If you can capture some of these stories on audio or video tape, you've hit a gold mine. It is a precious record indeed, preserving not only the actual words of a family legend but also the tone of voice, stops and starts, figures of speech, body gestures, and facial expressions of your storyteller. Books are available to teach you to edit audio and video tape. You could produce a collection of your relatives' oral history and design a cover for it. In years to come, there will be nothing like it to preserve the living memory of previous generations.

Written History

Many genealogists hope to make their research results available to others by preparing a written family history. For some people, this means spending years writing an 800-page book. For others, it means jotting down a few anecdotes. The written result of family history research can take as many forms as there are genealogists. You can choose a style and form that fit your talents and the time and energy you're willing to spend on it.

Conventionally, a family history is a book that includes all the information found in a genealogical search, told in narrative form. It gives not only names and vital dates, but also where people moved to and from, and why. Included might be a description of the boat that brought a person's ancestors to America, or a list of the articles they brought with them from their native land. To spice it up, the writer might include some of the family's oral history, stating clearly which parts are legend and which are verifiable fact. A family history always begins with the researcher herself or himself and works backward to the earliest found generation.

Some books are listed at the end of this chapter to help you write a family history. These sources offer help in organization, writing style, and grammar and the proper way to report genealogical information.

Writing a book is a pretty daunting prospect for most people, so many family historians find it best to start smaller. This is where you can get creative and invent writing projects related to your genealogy work. Following are a few ideas:

- Write a collection of family legends as told to you by your relatives. Include at the start of each one a summary of the facts you've found about the ancestors involved.
- Write a one-paragraph description of everyone on your family tree, based on information from your research. Then write a one-page description of each family group you've researched. This is actually a sneaky way of beginning a family history, because it will provide you with a starting point for writing something longer about your whole family.
- Choose one ancestor who particularly interests you and write a short biography of him or her. This would include vital statistics as well as information about the person's family, career, education, military service. If possible, weave in aspects of the ancestor's personality, which you can learn about through family stories, diaries, letters, an obituary, and other sources.
- Choose one event in the history of your family and turn it into a short story. This is especially fun if you do some reading about the place and time of the event. Maybe it would be the story of how your great-great-grandparents took a train from Philadelphia to Chicago after they married. You can learn about the transcontinental railway, what the Midwest was like at the time, what people wore—the more details of history you have to play with, the more fun it will be to write.

You can make any historical writing you do even nicer by

illustrating it. If you are linked to a coat of arms, you might include your family crest, along with a paragraph explaining what each symbol stands for. If you are of Scottish heritage, you could include a picture of your tartan. It is always good to draw your family tree or pedigree chart right into your family history, so a reader can refer to it along the way. Photographs are always a great way to illustrate. They can be copies of old photos of ancestors or pictures you or relatives have taken of houses or heirlooms belonging to your kin.

Whatever you write or prepare using your genealogical research, be sure to share it with your family, especially those who cooperated in your search. They will be delighted to have this unique keepsake of their family's past. Try not to take it personally if some relatives offer criticism of your book, claiming that you got information wrong. Instead be glad to get hints that some of your sources should be double-checked. If you turn out to be right after all, chalk their versions up to the quirks of oral history. They're only trying to get the record straight.

Computer Genealogy

Back in merry old England and in the early days of America, all documents were written in longhand. Noble lineages would be prepared by the king's professional calligraphers, while ordinary folks scrawled out their letters, wills, and family histories as best they could. That's hard to imagine, now that "cyberspace" has become a household word.

Today computers still play only a supporting role for most genealogists. The majority of researchers take notes by hand at libraries and interviews, but they prepare their written histories and biographies on a word processor. It's more convenient than a typewriter because you can correct easily, move text around, change to italic or boldface type, and perform other useful functions.

This is just the tip of the iceberg, though. For almost thirty years technology buffs have been developing software to assist in every aspect of family history. Now that the software has been improved to the point of performing well consistently, and people are getting used to working on computers, more and more genealogists have taken the plunge into high-tech ancestor searching.

The software packages are not the sort of thing you would find at your school's computer lab. Many of them are very expensive, and most need a fairly powerful personal computer to drive them (eight megabytes of RAM is recommended for most current products, although they will run—more slowly—on half that amount). Nevertheless, it is fun to see what's out there, and useful to keep it in mind for the future.

The pioneer in lineage software development was, not surprisingly, The Church of Jesus Christ of Latter-day Saints. The scholars in their Family History Library were dealing with so many millions of facts at any given time that staying on the cutting edge of organizational technology was a matter of survival. The resulting software, which continues to be updated and improved, is a package called Personal Ancestral File (PAF). Family Records is the main program in PAF. It is a storage system for data. You can enter vital information on your ancestors and Family Records will organize it for you and let you print it out in chart form. Today many companies have followed suit and introduced their own software for the genealogy market. Although most of it was originally designed for IBM/PC hardware, Macintosh versions are increasingly available. PAF is now complemented by CD-ROM technology. A vast array of censuses, vital records indexes, parish registers, and prepared family histories are available on CD.

PAF software is designed in accordance with a series of specifications called GEDCOM (Genealogical Data Communications). This generic file format was another brilliant invention by the people in Salt Lake City. It allows a genealogy file from any GEDCOM software system to be used in any other software system. If you buy software, look for GEDCOM compatibility, or you may find yourself wishing that you had. The point is to let people switch to a new system without having to start their files all over from scratch. It also lets family historians exchange files with one another.

Even in the computer age, genealogists still love to share information.

There are three main advantages of relying on computers for genealogy. The first is in entering information: You can enter data piecemeal as you get it and access it in many forms. Your computer (ideally) never misplaces a fact and automatically files information in a logical way so it's useful to you. It can also spare you from some of the duller tasks of genealogy. For example, if you are entering biographical information on a family, that family's place of residence may come up many times (moved to Tillytown, Sharon County, MI; married in Tillytown, Sharon County, MI; son born in Tillytown, Sharon County, MI). Software can allow you to program certain single keys to type out entire words. The town, county, and state needed could be entered in three keystrokes each time they are needed.

The second advantage of family history software is in organization. Software packages come with de facto organizational systems that will classify any piece of data you enter. If through experience you decide you want to organize in another way, current software allows you to make such changes. For example, you may decide that being able to call up data by surname is not enough. Then you can program your computer to access information by an event's date or location.

The most spectacular contribution of computer software is output. All the software packages include printing programs for family group sheets, pedigree charts, and family trees, which will print out complete with scanned images of your ancestors.

With a combination of graphics technology, desktop publishing software, and scanners, it is possible to produce a gorgeous family history book with your very own mouse and keyboard (and a top-notch printer, of course). Coats of arms are available on disk, and photos of your relatives can be scanned in and digitally pasted into the book. You can even scan in old letters and documents to illustrate your text with facsimiles of your ancestors' handwriting.

Preserve Your Own History

Whether you use PAF and a laser printer, or a typewriter and a felt-tip drawing pen, you are making an important contribution to the future. By carefully collecting and preserving your family's past, you are acting as a custodian for information that might otherwise be lost forever.

There is even more you can do. As you try genealogical research, you will experience frustration over what is not there. You will wish that your grandmother's attic contained diaries and letters written by every one of your ancestors, so you could get a clearer idea of what they were like.

Now is your chance to make a record of your own life, so that, in a few generations, your descendants can find that record and really feel that they know you. Start a diary and write in it as often as you can. Keep report cards, photographs (label and date the backs), prizes from school, printed programs from concerts you enjoyed. You could even write notes on them explaining what you liked especially.

You could begin an ongoing autobiography. Start with your vital statistics. What are your earliest memories? Who taught each grade of school, and what classes did you love or hate? Does your family move around a lot? What does your house look like? Who is your best friend? What important events happened in each year? Also write down everything you know about your parents and siblings.

The past is always a hard thing to grasp. As you learn by doing family history research, it is difficult to understand what everyday life was like when your parents were growing up, let alone in seventeenth-century Scotland. Even your own past fades from your memory very quickly. Keeping a record of your adventures and feelings will remind you of them in years to come when they are no longer so clear in your mind.

In a hundred years that record will be a real treasure to young people learning to trace their family roots.

Resources

PREPARING YOUR WRITTEN FAMILY HISTORY

Fletcher, William P. *Record Your Family History.* Berkeley, CA: Ten Speed Press, 1989.

This is a guide to preserving your family's oral history on videotape and audiotape. It suggests interview techniques and sample questions, as well as giving examples of what to listen for in your relatives' stories.

Jordan, Lewis. *Cite Your Sources: A Manual for Documenting Family Histories and Genealogical Records.* Jackson, MS: University Press of Mississippi: 1980.

If you don't cite sources correctly in your family history, there is no way a reader can be sure that your work is accurate. This book gives standard, clear citation advice for sources from birth certificates to gravestones.

McLaughlin, Paul. *A Family Remembers.* North Vancouver, BC: Self-Counsel Press, 1993.

This is an excellent up-to-date guide on how to create a family memoir using video cameras and tape recorders. Includes advice on interviewing, acoustics, lighting, scripts, and editing.

Shull, Wilma Sadler. *Photographing Your Heritage.* Salt Lake City: Ancestry Publishing, 1989.

A good introduction to using even the simplest camera to record artifacts in your own home. Photographs of relatives, their houses, and their heirlooms make an excellent way to illustrate your family history.

Shumway, Gary L. and Hartley, William G. *An Oral History Primer.* Salt Lake City: Shumway, 1973.

The author gives examples of how collected oral histories can shed light on your family's heritage. He offers advice on how to get your relatives to tell tales and sing songs into your tape recorder, and what to do with them once you've collected them.

FAMILY HISTORY ON COMPUTER

American Genealogical Lending Library (AGLL)
801-298-5446

Call this number to search their electronic databases by phone. A few censuses are available for sale on CD-ROM and marriage records on floppy disk.

Ancestral File Operations Unit
50 East North Temple Street
Salt Lake City, UT 84150
801-240-2584

Write for information on the Family History Library's famous Personal Ancestral File software and the GEDCOM compatibility system.

Banner Blue Software
P.O. Box 7865
Fremont, CA 94537
510-795-4490

Write for information on the Biography Maker software. A program designed to narrow your focus as you write your family history, it allows you to write one ancestor's story at a time and helps you tie several stories together with writing and history aids. For IBM.

Clifford, Karen. *Genealogy and Computers for the Complete Beginner.* Baltimore: Genealogical Publishing, 1992.

This is a textbook, complete with quizzes and exercises,

to enable the novice to apply new concepts in genealogical research.

Commsoft, Inc.
7795 Bell Road
P.O. Box 310
Windsor, CA 95495-0130

Write for information on their Roots IV software, which features a unique flexibility in its data entry program.

Dollarhide Systems
203 Holly Street
Bellingham, WA 28225
801-298-5358

Write for information on Everyone's Family Tree software. This program is particularly easy for beginners.

Genealogical Computing

For the most up-to-date information on technology in ancestry hunting, turn to this periodical from Ancestry Publishing, Salt Lake City, UT.

Interlock Software Systems
P.O. Box 130953
Houston, TX 77219
713-680-8576

Write for information on Generations Library Software.

LDB Association Inc.
Dept. Q, Box 20837
Wichita, KS 67208-6837
316-683-6200

Write for information on KinWrite and KinPublish software.

Quinsept, Inc.
P.O. Box 216
Lexington, MA 02173
1-800-637-ROOT

Call (toll-free) or write for information on Family Roots and Lineage software.

Pence, Richard A. *Computer Genealogy: A Guide to Research Through High Technology.* **Salt Lake City: Ancestry, 1991.**

An excellent, solid introduction to the concept of using computers for family history. Although a few years old, all the basics still hold. Also, all the software the author discusses is still in use, but in more advanced versions.

The Internet

More and more genealogists, both beginners and pros, are surfing the Net for information and good conversation. Catch the wave! Services include chat boards, frequented by researchers looking for specific information, as well as troubleshooting forums sponsored by some of the major software manufacturers. Ask your librarian for help.

Glossary

aristocracy A group of people with exceptional rank or privileges.

chieftain A leader of a group or clan.

conversion Change from one religion to another.

credo A statement of essential beliefs.

cryptic Intentionally puzzling or mysterious.

druidism The religion or rites of the Druids, members of an ancient Celtic priesthood.

edict A judicial decision.

egalitarian Believing in human equality in social, political, and economic affairs.

entrepreneur One who organizes a business or enterprise.

gazetteer A geographical dictionary.

gentry In England, the class of people between the nobility and farmers.

gumshoe Detective.

heirloom A piece of personal property passed on by inheritance.

heretical Adhering to an opinion that goes against a religion's dogma.

inalienable Incapable of being surrendered.

incumbent The holder of an office or position.

indigenous Innate to a particular area.

mystical Relating to a direct knowledge of God.

pagan A person or group who does not believe in the God of the Bible.

parish A church district in the care of one pastor.

roguish Dishonest or mischievous.

sept A group of people believing themselves descended from a common ancestor.

sordid Morally degraded.

stalwart Strong, uncompromising.

Index

ABOUT THE AUTHOR
Anne E. Johnson holds a degree from the University of Wisconsin. She has spent many years researching and performing traditional ballads and songs from the British Isles and Ireland. This work inspired her interest in British history and emigration and in her own British roots.

ILLUSTRATION CREDITS
Cover, © G & M. David de Lossy/The Image Bank; cover inset and pp. 3, 4, 6, 7, 9, 24, 27, 45, 46, 48, 50, 55, 56, 58, 84, 95, 140, 142, BETTMAN. Color insert: p. 2, London Pictures Service; pp. 3, 11, BETTMAN; pp. 4, 5, 6, 7, 10, 12, 13: courtesy of the British Tourist Authority; p. 8, © Sheila Gray/Format; pp. 9, 15, © Roshini Kempadoo/Format; p. 14, © Ulrike Preuss/Format; p. 16, © Larry Dale Gordon/The Image Bank.

LAYOUT AND DESIGN
Kim Sonsky